GROWING
SLOW
BIBLE STUDY

GROWING SLOW

BIBLE STUDY

A 6-WEEK GUIDED JOURNEY TO UN-HURRYING YOUR HEART

JENNIFER DUKES LEE

BETHANYHOUSE

a division of Baker Publishing Group
Minneapolis, Minnesota

Published by Bethany House Publishers
11400 Hampshire Avenue South
Bloomington, Minnesota 55438
www.bethanyhouse.com

Bethany House Publishers is a division of
Baker Publishing Group, Grand Rapids, Michigan

Printed in the United States of America

Library of Congress Cataloging-in-Publication Data
Names: Lee, Jennifer Dukes, author.
Title: Growing slow Bible study : a 6-week guided journey to un-hurrying your heart / Jennifer Dukes Lee.
Description: Minneapolis, Minnesota : Bethany House Publishers, a division of Baker Publishing Group, [2021] | Includes bibliographical references.
Identifiers: LCCN 2020052774 | ISBN 9780764238369 (paperback) | ISBN 9781493431649 (ebook)
Subjects: LCSH: Lee, Jennifer Dukes. Growing slow. | Peace of mind—Religious aspects—Christianity—Textbooks. | Stress management for women—Textbooks. | Rhythm—Religious aspects—Christianity—Textbooks.
Classification: LCC BV4908.5 .L443 2021 | DDC 248.8/43—dc23
LC record available at https://lccn.loc.gov/2020052774

Author represented by Alive Literary Agency

21 22 23 24 25 26 27   7 6 5 4 3 2 1

Contents

Introduction

Slowing down: Is it even possible in this age?

Every year I cross paths with thousands of women—in person and in my inbox. Each comes from different stations and stages of life. But it seems none is immune from the itch to hurry.

Teen girls feel rushed to make decisions about their futures, while juggling overloaded calendars and crazy schedules.

Young-adult women, just starting out on their own, worry that they are falling behind—before they even get started—when they compare themselves to their peers.

Middle-aged women race to do more, juggling responsibilities at home and at work, and they ask themselves, *Shouldn't I be further along by now?*

And older women—even those who have lived rich, full lives—wonder how the years seem to fly by faster than ever before. They ask themselves, *Where did the time go? Did I do enough with the time I've been given? What will be my legacy?*

The story is the same for all of us: We feel the pressure to hurry. We feel this urge to constantly check our phones, to monitor our progress, and to wonder if we should be further along than we are. We are weary from our frantic-paced living. Our hearts are squeezed. This accelerated lifestyle affects our sleep, our mood, our relationships, and our ability to truly appreciate the beautiful, everyday gifts from God.

What if we could finally slow down? What if we could truly live in the *now*?

I have good news for you. It's not too late to slow it all down and really *live* your life instead of hustle through it.

And it's not too early, either.

No matter your age or season of life, Jesus is calling you to something better than hurry.

I know what some of you are thinking: *Slow down? That's not possible. There's too much at stake, too much to be done. I don't want to miss an opportunity. I can't afford to slow down.*

But let me ask you this: What if you can't afford *not* to?

That's the question I began to ask myself when it was clear that my hurried existence was taking a toll on my soul—and my body. The problem wasn't just a busy schedule. The cure would require more than excusing myself from a set of obligations.

I needed to un-hurry my heart.

Do you have a hurried heart, too?

See if this sounds familiar: A hurried heart is the anxious way you feel when you calculate all that must be done. It's the weight on your chest when you think you've got to hustle. It's the pressure to catch up with everyone else. And it's the condition that makes you falsely believe that the small, good things you're growing really aren't that great after all.

We need a rescue to calm our hurried hearts.

And that's exactly what God offers. Throughout the Bible, God shows us what it looks like to find peace in a chaotic world. His words give us clear direction on how to find satisfaction in the here and now. His Son, Jesus, demonstrates how to live a slower-paced, intentional life. Jesus took time to connect, not only with his Father, but with the people all around him.

I know how an un-hurried way of life can feel out of reach. Patterns of hurry are ingrained into our thinking, and it may take a little work to untangle ourselves from old habits. But look at you right now! When you picked up this study guide, you took the first step toward a slower, better way.

So gather up some friends and join me on our fifth-generation family farm, a place where I have learned the ancient art of Growing Slow. Together, we'll learn an un-hurried way of life.

This Bible study will open a path for you, leading you away from the pressures of bigger, harder, faster. My prayer for you is that when you reach the last page of this study, you will find the true relief that comes when you stop running and start resting in Jesus.

It is possible.

Ready, set, slow.

Jennifer

How to Get the Most out of This Study

Along with this workbook, each person will need a pen or pencil and the following:

1. **A Bible.** I quote from the New International Version unless otherwise noted. If you don't have that version, you can find the text on a website, such as www.BibleGateway.com, or in a smartphone app.

2. **My book *Growing Slow* (Zondervan, 2021).** The book is not a required tool, but a strong recommendation. The book provides a framework for the study and cements key concepts while helping you apply them in your everyday life.

   At the beginning of each session, I list chapters in *Growing Slow* that correlate to the material in this workbook. As you read, I encourage you to highlight phrases that resonate with you. Take note of concepts that seem surprising, challenging, or relatable to you.

3. **A commitment to complete each session.** In any study, we have two choices: Go all in, or simply go through the motions. Decide today that you will go all in. Of course, life happens. Schedules change. New commitments arise. But you will grow most if you

- ask God to reveal his heart to you as you respond to the questions and prompts
- be honest with God and yourself as you engage with the material
- put into practice what Scripture asks of you
- embrace the adventure!

HERE'S WHAT YOU'LL FIND IN EACH WEEK'S STUDY

The Growing Slow Bible Study is divided into six sessions to follow the pattern of the growing season: Cultivate, Plant, Grow, Harvest, Celebrate, and Heal. Here's what you will find in each of the sessions:

A key Bible verse: Each passage relates to that week's content.

My Land: Much of the study centers on lessons learned from the land, through Scripture. In the My Land section, I go first by sharing my struggles right here on our land in rural Iowa.

Your Land: Here, you'll have an opportunity to get honest about your struggles in the land where you dwell.

The Holy Land: The land is more than a backdrop to the biblical narrative. It is a critical part of the story. Each week, we'll return to the Holy Land to learn and grow alongside our spiritual ancestors.

Un-Hurry Your Heart: This is an opportunity to reflect on the week's lessons and apply them to everyday life.

Prayer: We end each lesson by asking God to sink his truths deep within us. Whether you pray in a group or on your own, your conversations with God have power to yield change in your life.

ESPECIALLY FOR LEADERS

I put together a short leader's guide to help you facilitate a group study. The guide includes tips and ideas to take the guesswork out of leading a group. See page 121 for the guide.

CULTIVATE

TURNING OVER THE SOIL OF YOUR HEART

The Lord is not slow in keeping his promise, as some understand slowness. Instead he is patient with you, not wanting anyone to perish, but everyone to come to repentance.

2 Peter 3:9

WEEK 1 FOCUS

- to identify how hurry hurts the human heart
- to understand the importance of preparation and patience

LET'S GET STARTED

Read the introduction and chapters 1 and 2 of *Growing Slow.*

Watch a free teaching video from Jennifer based on this week's session. Visit www.GrowingSlowBook.com/Resources to find the video. When prompted, enter this code for access: JDLGrowingSlow.

Why did you decide to take the Growing Slow journey? What do you most hope to gain by the time you reach the last page?

I felt called to this book because I saw Aarti from Food Network mention it and it spoke to me. It made me feel like it was something I needed because i've always felt like a late bloomer of life and I felt like this book would help me to appreciate my slow journey and even relish in it. By the end I just want to have my faith and relationship w/ God to feel stronger and trust Him and the pace he's had me grow at.

MY LAND

Confession: Some of the worst moments of my life have happened while I was going too fast.

I'm not talking about the speeding tickets—there have been a few. Or the time, in my typical rush, I knocked the water glass to the floor, shattering it into a thousand pieces. Little casualties like those litter the freeway that has been my life.

I'm talking about bigger things—the way that, in a hurry, I have cut short meaningful conversations with broken-down people who needed me to hear their heart. The times when I have nagged my kids, clenched my teeth at the people I love most, or shut someone down with the body language of a turned shoulder, all because I was running late.

I was at my worst when I was a young mom. I would fantasize about how I might be able to coordinate the kids' naps for *just forty-five minutes* so I could squeeze in some writing—as if those forty-five minutes were the *real* work I was called to do.

I thought my breakneck speed would be cured when we moved to my husband's fifth-generation farm in Iowa. The pace here is easy. Traffic is often slowed, not by a tangled knot of cars at rush hour but by a slow-moving tractor or a cow that found a weak spot in the fence. Life on the farm is marked by seasons—cultivating, growing, planting, and harvest.

People have this romantic idea that because we live under a wide-open sky, our lives are slower paced.

But the truth is—like almost everyone I know—we succumb to the enchantments of faster, bigger, stronger.

Like almost everyone I know, we dismiss the wonder of ordinary life. Deep down, we desire sustainable growth, but we can't quite shake the allure of "more" and "fast."

I get tempted to order life around achievement and hustle, which leaves me anxious, weary, overwhelmed, and tense. Many times, I have wondered if I am doing enough to grow good things in my life.

As a result, I have suffered from what I call "a hurried heart."

A hurried heart can be defined as a state of hastiness and rushing that leaves you feeling agitated, anxious, ragged, and restless. When suffering from a hurried heart, it can be difficult to believe that slowing down is an option.

There is no pill or magic cure to fix a hurried heart. As I wrote in *Growing Slow*, the cure is "an inside job."

It starts here . . . by making a commitment to grow slow.

YOUR LAND

The theme for Session 1 is cultivate. On many farms, the soil is cultivated—when the topsoil is turned over completely—before seeds are planted.

Farmers cultivate soil. God cultivates hearts.

God wants to "turn over" the soil of your heart so that he can plant seeds that produce good growth. One way to cultivate the heart is through honest self-reflection.

Let's get courageous. Let's slow down and cultivate.

When was the last time you felt like your heart was hurried?

How pervasive is hurry in our culture? Is it getting worse or better?

With all of the gadgets, hacks, and technology available to help us get more done at a faster pace, why are people so frazzled?

On the line below, mark the place that best reflects the state of your heart.

|———————+————————+————————+————————|
0   25   50   75   100

   0   At the breaking point

  25   Hurried and pressured

  50   Hurried, but managing it decently

  75   Have learned the art of slowing down, but need help staying the course

100   Un-hurried, calm, and peaceful

To understand the toll of hurry, take an inventory of how you feel—and what you do—when you have a hurried heart. Put an X in the box next to the sentences that feel true for you.

☐ When I wake up, I immediately check my phone.

☐ I don't remember the last time I felt bored.

☐ I multitask but feel like nothing is getting done.

☐ I get frustrated in traffic or long lines at the store.

☐ I feel a sense of urgency to get things done.

☐ I feel guilty because I know that I don't make time for daily conversations with God.

☐ Periods of slowness make me uneasy.

☐ I feel like I should have more to show for my life.

☐ I am not sleeping well because of my racing mind.

☐ I am not eating well because of all that's on my mind.

☐ I compare myself to others and feel I'm falling short.

☐ I rarely take time to stop and smell the proverbial roses.

Friend, it takes courage to admit our struggles. But that's where true change in the Growing Slow journey begins.

One of the biggest drivers of a hurried heart is this idea that "I should be further along by now." We look at our lives and discount the good things we are growing because the growth is sometimes small or unseen. It isn't as fruitful as we hoped. We wonder why we aren't having more influence on others, more success, more money, more comfort, more progress in our marriages, more fruit in our parenting. The list is lengthy.

Here's a list of areas where women often wish they were seeing more growth, faster. Circle the ones that strike you personally.

career

side hustle

finances

personal productivity

marriage or dating life

my children

grades

my weight-loss plan

exercise goals

friendships

my faith life

personal development

hobbies

overcoming sinful behavior

recovering from a bad habit or addiction

other: _____

Naturally, we want to grow good things. That is a worthy aim. We can engage in all sorts of self-help practices to promote good growth—taking a college class, buying a recommended book, seeking the advice of a mentor, practicing good habits, and much more. Those are healthy activities that will promote growth in many areas you circled above, in the same way that watering a garden promotes growth.

But it can be easy to forget that the pace of that growth ultimately does not rest in our hands or on the pages of a self-help book.

How can I be so sure about that? Open your Bible to 1 Corinthians 3:7 and fill in the blanks:

So neither the one who plants nor the one who waters is anything, but only

_____ , _____ _____ .

Maybe you feel behind. Maybe you feel like growth is slow in your life. Make no mistake: There is more going on underneath the surface of the soil than you can imagine.

Let's get digging.

HOLY LAND

The truth is, the slowness of God doesn't sit well with most people. His pace can feel exasperating. Who out there enjoys waiting on the Lord when you wanted results or answers yesterday?

Anyone?

Hmm, I don't see a single hand.

Our spiritual ancestors can relate. Over the next six sessions, we will return to the Holy Land, learning lessons from the people who roamed there.

We will also zero in on the land itself. A fascinating aspect of the Christian faith is that our belief system is not an ethereal or abstract concept. Rather, God met real people in real times and places. I have never visited the Holy Land, but many of my friends have. They say that because of their visit, the Scriptures came alive in a new way.

If I could, I'd charter a plane, and we'd all go there together. But since that's not possible, we'll journey there through the Bible.

I am so excited to enter this beautiful and chosen land, which opens up to us in vivid ways in Scripture. These first steps are foundational to the Growing Slow journey because we are all shaped by place, and we can't fully understand our personal story until we know the collective stories and places from which we originate.

So let's begin with a whirlwind tour of the biblical land, starting at the very beginning and progressing forward along the timeline of biblical history. Read the following verses and fill in the blanks.

In the beginning God created the heavens and the _____.

Genesis 1:1

I am going to bring floodwaters on the _____ to destroy all life under the heavens, every creature that has the breath of life in it. Everything on _____ will perish.

Genesis 6:17

All the animals and all the creatures that move along the ground and all the birds—everything that moves on _____—came out of the ark, one kind after another.

Genesis 8:19

The LORD had said to Abram, "Go from your country, your people and your father's household to the _____ I will show you."

Genesis 12:1

Pharaoh said to Joseph, "Your father and your brothers have come to you, and the land of Egypt is before you; settle your father and your brothers in the best part of the _____. Let them live in Goshen.

Genesis 47:5–6

So I have come down to rescue them from the hand of the Egyptians and to bring them up out of that _____ into a good and spacious _____, a _____ flowing with milk and honey.

Exodus 3:8

So Joshua took the entire _____, just as the LORD had directed Moses, and he gave it as an inheritance to Israel according to their tribal divisions. Then the _____ had rest from war.

Joshua 11:23

What's the common word or words you wrote in the provided spaces?

Every blank you filled above is represented by the Hebrew word *eretz*. That's the Hebrew word for *land* or *earth*. It is the fifth most frequently used noun in the Hebrew Bible, after the Hebrew words for *Lord*, *son*, *God*, and *king*.[1]

What does that suggest to you about the land and its frequent inclusion in the Bible?

May I share my personal answer to that question? I think it suggests that the land is more than a backdrop for biblical history. Rather, the land is a significant character in the magnificent biblical narrative from the very beginning. There are more than two thousand instances of this word *eretz* in the Old Testament.

In the first sentence of the Bible, God creates the earth, *eretz*. A few days later, in the world's first garden, he bends down to earth, scoops up a fistful of dirt, breathes into it, and creates a living being (Genesis 2:7). After sin enters the world, everything on the land falls apart, and it gets worse with each turned page. Floodwaters rise to cover the whole earth. God spares only Noah, his family, and pairs of all the animals.

All hope is not lost. God's covenantal promise to his people is centered around—you guessed it—land. It goes something like this: The Israelites escape *land*, to spend a solid forty years roaming around *land*, weaving an uncharted path toward *land*—the promised *land*, a *land* "flowing with milk and honey" (Exodus 3:8 and a whole bunch of other places).

It's no wonder that scholars often refer to the land of Israel as "the fifth gospel." We would miss a beautiful part of God's message if we muted the land.

Land's lessons don't end in the Old Testament. Jesus drew lessons from the land that were so clear to a first-century agrarian culture. We don't want to miss those lessons in this modern age—lessons found in vineyards, wheat, threshing floors, gleaning, fields for grazing, and soil. Rain signaled God's provision. Literal droughts tested the faith of people. Jesus was known not only as the true vine, but also as the Good Shepherd.

Let's dig deeper by reading the following verses and pondering the work of God's hand, taking note of . . .

. . . how he can grow something big out of something quite small. **Read Matthew 13:31–32 and record any observations.**

. . . how you, along with all creation, are known and fully his. **Read Psalm 50:11–12 and record any observations.**

. . . how God is truly in control of the earth and all that dwells upon it, including you. **Read Job 12:7–10 and record any observations.**

All through history, God shows his care for his earth and his people by tending carefully to them, as he grows good things slowly. As the old song says, "He's got the whole world in his hands."

God, who holds the whole world in his hands,

who causes the mustard seed to grow,

who hangs stars in a velvet sky,

who tells the ocean how far to go,
who summons light,
who makes shadows long,
who oversees storehouses of snow,
who knows every grain of sand,
who counts feathers and moves mountains,
who bursts forth in bloom,
who is fire and wind,
whisper and thunder,
resurrection power and King over all,
who holds all things together . . .
he also holds you and all the good things you're growing.

UN-HURRY YOUR HEART

So far this session, we've gotten honest with ourselves about areas where we feel hurried. We've admitted how God sometimes moves slower than we prefer. And in the last section, we established that God teaches key principles about the ancient art of Growing Slow through lessons of the land.

Now it's time to apply lessons to our own lives as we move toward our goal of un-hurrying our hearts.

Briefly, what does a hurried heart feel like for you? Write down a few hurried-heart symptoms that you've experienced—or have seen others experience:

Physical:

Emotional:

Mental:

Spiritual:

You're not alone. On page xv of *Growing Slow*, I write candidly about my struggle.

My body, this scaffolding that carries me along life's journey, began to desta-bilize. I became fearful that my ready-set-go pace would kill me—maybe not physically, but emotionally, mentally, and, perhaps, spiritually. . . . I simply couldn't carry it all as I ran around like a crazy person trying to make some kind of difference in the world. Worst of all, I knew that I wasn't fully pres-ent for the best moments unfolding around me. I wasn't sure I even liked the person I had become.

Like you, I needed God to un-hurry my heart. As we take this jour-ney together, we will consider the seasonal cycle of growth and nature's rhythms. If you spent a year with me on our farm, you would see the whole growing cycle in motion in fields of corn and soybeans—from spring planting, to summer growth, to autumn harvest, and then, to the restful reflection of winter.

But before the planting comes a key first step.

Read Proverbs 28:19. What did the author say needed to be done to the land to assure the abundance of a later harvest?

Depending on which version of the Bible you are using, the verse indicated that you needed to "work the land" or till it to assure good growth.

In modern farming practices, not all farmers "till" or cultivate their land, preferring instead the benefits of "no-till farming." But the concept of cultivating remains an important metaphor as we prepare our hearts for un-hurried living and sustainable growth. God is earth's first Farmer, and he is interested in cultivating our hearts, preparing our "soil" before planting seeds in us.

Cultivation promotes good growth by preparing the seedbed. Oftentimes, behind the cultivator and tractor, a rake will smooth out the ground and break up clods. My husband calls cultivation a "burying of the past," because last year's growth is flipped over, and fresh earth is brought forth.

Metaphorically, we often think of "cultivating" in gentle, almost maternal ways. We carefully cultivate friendships or a child's talents, for example. But, in fact, cultivation is a complete upheaval. Everything must be flipped upside down.

One way God turns our heart-soil over is through periods of repentance.

When we "grow slow," we give God the time he desires to dig underneath the surface, unearthing the stuff that we don't like to think about, let alone admit to ourselves or others.

In other words: we've got to face our sin.

I know how hard it is to deal with The Heavy. But like my husband says, we have to bury the past. That doesn't mean we don't *deal* with the past. Quite the opposite. A farmer knows that he has to get the plow dirty, moving through every square of his field to turn the land inside out. Without this, the crops may not grow like he wants them to.

Now, imagine God on the seat of the tractor. He wants to cover every square inch of your heart.

As you consider the field of your heart, consider these questions:

What does God want to cultivate in you?

What area of your life needs to be "turned over"?

What sin(s) do you know you must repent in order to promote sustainable growth in your life?

Talk to God about your answers to those questions, and take your time with that important first step of the Growing Slow journey. This is called the *Growing Slow Bible Study* for a reason. You are allowed to take the time you need—minutes, hours, or even days. It will be time well spent.

My prayer is that, as you return to this page, your heart feels lighter and freer. Good things grow in a cultivated field. "Turning over" the soil of our hearts is not a once-and-done effort. My prayer is that, each day, we take the time necessary to let God unearth the stuff that doesn't belong in our hearts.

One of the biggest barriers to repentance is hurry. We are in a rush to get things done, move on to the next things, and not truly tend to the soil of our hearts.

But cultivation takes time. Sometimes it's painful. Quite often, cultivation can feel like a lengthy trip through the wilderness, especially when we are eager to see growth in our fields.

The Israelites could relate to the painfulness of slow growth.

Read Deuteronomy 2:7. Fill in the blanks.

The Lord your God has blessed you in all the work of your hands. He has watched over your journey through this _____. These _____ years the Lord your God has been with you, and you have not lacked anything.

Reread the last sentence. What did the Israelites lack during their wilderness journey?

God walked his people through a great wilderness on their journey into the promised land, a land of milk and honey.

Surely, the journey from the wilderness to the promised land must have felt exasperatingly slow, as days turned into months and years.

It was, for sure, a Growing Slow journey. But they never lacked a thing.

Read Deuteronomy 31:6, Exodus 33:14, and Joshua 1:5. What do these verses reveal about God's whereabouts during that long, slow journey?

On their Growing Slow journey, the Israelites found God to be faithful and trustworthy. God was always on time with food, water, and protection from enemies. At times, God will go slow for your protection. Sometimes, he'll go slow to show his provision. And other times, he'll go slow for preparation. That's how it worked for the Israelites, and that's how it works for us. This is the important work of cultivation—learning to trust the One who is in charge of the growth.

If you're like most people, you want things faster, sooner, easier. But life isn't a reality TV competition, where someone is suddenly "discovered" in front of a live audience.

As I reflect on God's cultivating work in me, I believe that the quality of the fruit I produce is directly proportional to the time God takes to shape me.

Good fruit takes time! How have you found that to be true in your life?

Before God grows good things *through* us, he wants to grow good things *in* us. God is cultivating us so our lives bear important fruit, such as obedience, integrity, patience, perseverance, and good habits. God is shaping us into the women we are becoming.

He can do more in his slowness than we can ever do in our hurry.

GOD CAN DO MORE IN HIS SLOWNESS THAN WE CAN EVER DO IN OUR HURRY.

Read our key verse for this week's session, 2 Peter 3:9. Fill in the blanks.

The Lord is not _____ in keeping his promise, as some understand _____. Instead he is _____ _____ , not wanting anyone to perish, but everyone to come to repentance.

Keep that verse in mind as you flip back to the list on page 18. In that list, you identified areas where you wish you could see more growth.

What does 2 Peter 3:9 suggest about what's happening under the soil, in a dark place where only God can see?

As we close our first session, let's pay attention to the land under our feet. God has you where you are for a reason—to cultivate goodness in your own little corner of the world.

If you're able, step outside right now and notice God at work in the world, growing beautiful things that he alone caused to flourish.

God consistently brings sunlight, rain, the cool of night, the shade of a tree, the haze of the moon, reliably waxing and waning. There is a certainty of God's presence in all seasons. In this wild world, I need that certainty.

After you step outside, record any observations about God's care, the place he has you right now, or anything else he brings to mind. If you are unable to go outside, think about a time when you encountered the love and sovereignty of God through nature. Write your response below.

PRAYER

Let's pray that, over the next several weeks, God will reveal areas where he wants to cultivate us. Let's also pray that he gives us the courage to slow down. We don't have to hustle in order to bear good fruit.

Fill in the lines of the following prayer with areas where you need God's help.

Dear Lord,

From the moment you knelt down in the Garden of Eden and cupped dirt in your hands, you decided that I—along with every other human being on earth—am worth it. I am worth the time that you take to cultivate my heart. I confess that I am sometimes in a hurry, prone to distraction, and don't like to wait for your hand to move. I also confess that I don't always take the time to deal with the unrepentant sin in my life. Today, I confess these areas of my life to you:

....

....

....

....

....

....

Your word says that you are not slow in keeping your promises, as some understand slowness. Help me to live in the promise that you will grow things in your will, in your way, and in your timing. In Jesus' name, amen.

PLANT

BECOMING A GOOD SOIL GIRL IN A FAST-PACED WORLD

You are God's field.

1 Corinthians 3:9

WEEK 2 FOCUS

- to gain a clearer understanding of the condition of your heart
- to discover how you can love life more when you let God be God

LET'S GET STARTED

Read chapters 3 and 6 of *Growing Slow*. (Optional: chapters 4 and 5.)

Watch a free teaching video from Jennifer based on this week's session. Visit www.GrowingSlowBook.com/Resources to find the video. When prompted, enter this code for access: JDLGrowingSlow.

We ended our last session with a prayer, asking God to help us live in his promise that he will grow good things in our lives—in his will, his way, and his timing. We asked for his help in surrendering areas where we have been tempted to run ahead of God.

How has this awareness affected you in the past week? Have you noticed changes in how you act and react? Where have you been aware of symptoms of a hurried heart?

It can be challenging to tap the brakes and suddenly slow down, even when we know we should. We have obligations and deadlines. We are eager to see growth. As we consider life priorities—in our work, fitness, health, relationships, spiritual formation, and more—it can be tempting to want immediate results. But there *is* a way to slow down and trust God with the seeds we're planting. There *is* a way to discover how truly fulfilling life can be—when we let God be God. I'm ready to give it a try. How about you?

This week, we'll focus on developing a relationship of trust with the earth's very first Farmer, God himself. The Divine Farmer has a remarkable field that he wants to plant. The Bible lets us know exactly what that field is.

Read today's theme verse (1 Corinthians 3:9) and write down the identity of the field.

You, my friend, are a field—a precious, wild, and wonderful field planted by the hand of God.

And that's not all. God is preparing you to do some planting, too, in the cultivated fields where you live and breathe and move.

Let's plant.

MY LAND

My parents recently entered their eighties and celebrated their sixtieth wedding anniversary. As an extended family, we made a point of celebrating those milestones together.

I realize how blessed I am to have parents who have lived long, fruitful lives with a marriage spanning decades. When I sat at the table during Mom's birthday party, I looked around the room and saw the sweet gift of persevering—kids and grandkids laughing and eating cake, longtime friends walking through the door to offer greetings. All around us was evidence of deep-rooted living and sustainable growth—*and how that can only happen over time.*

Sitting there, I thought about the expectations my parents must have had early in marriage. As they planted those first seeds, they had ambition, dreams, and eagerness. They wouldn't have expected all the trials—and there were many. They have faced health struggles: cancer, heart-bypass surgery, an amputation. They moved frequently, endured many struggles, recessions, the loss of loved ones, disagreements, and more. I wonder if they would have persevered past the wedding altar if they had been given a crystal ball to see all the struggles they would face. Honestly, they may not have had kids if they had had a preview of all the sleepless nights the four of us kids surely brought upon them!

But hindsight tells a different story. My parents assure me that they wouldn't have had it any other way. They can now see so much of their life in a way that I cannot yet see mine: in reverse. They are still planting seeds, for sure, but at the same time, they are seeing the rich harvest from seeds planted long ago.

Their life bears testimony to what I have only begun to learn: People are slow grown! Spiritual growth takes time, raising kids into maturity takes time, building a business takes time, forging deep friendships takes time.

PEOPLE ARE SLOW GROWN!

I have made my choice to live a Growing Slow life, and I submit to the idea of being a slow-grown woman. I talk about my choice on page 33 of *Growing Slow*:

> I didn't want to be the kind of mom who misses her daughter's one-minute moment to shine on the court because I was answering an email from a women's conference leader. I didn't want to be the kind of friend who isn't

fully present when we're out for dinner. . . . I no longer wanted to dismiss the quotidian and unseen moments because of external pressure to dream a bigger dream.

In short, I want to plant my seeds, let God grow them, and enjoy my life instead of racing through it. I don't want to live my life as if I'm afraid of being late to my own funeral.[1]

YOUR LAND

Describe a time when you planted a seed in something or someone (such as a friend, a child, a business, a personal development goal) and felt exasperated by the time it took to see real results.

In the My Land section, I shared how the fullness of growth in my extended family could be viewed only after a lengthy period of time—in our case, over decades.

Where have you seen sustainable growth in your life, or the life of someone you know?

Consider everything you are planting in the fields of your life. Where do you most want to see growth that lasts a long time, perhaps outliving you?

Our culture is trained to want what we want *now*. Look to the ads for proof. Everyone is selling a quicker way to grow your business, lose weight, make a buck. We want quicker Internet connections and faster workouts with the same results.

We believe that hurry makes us more productive, more efficient. We value multitasking. But what if, in our rush, we are sacrificing quality?

The wise Solomon wrote, "A person in a hurry makes mistakes" (Proverbs 19:2 GW).

Let's examine five key reasons why we are in a hurry.

FIVE REASONS WE HURRY

Outside pressure. We feel pressure from a parent, a teacher, or a boss to get more done, hit a new milestone, or reach a new goal. If we are young, we may feel pressure to hurry up and find a spouse. If we are newly married, we may feel pressure to build a family. In our careers, we may feel societal pressure to make advancements quickly.

Unworthiness. For some, self-worth is linked to achievement. Worth is measured by productivity and benchmarks. If we place a high value on others' perceptions of us, we will hustle to prove ourselves to people.

Competition and comparison. We fear that if we don't keep up the pace, we will fall behind and everyone will pass us by. As we plant our fields, it can feel like the grass is greener on the other side of the fence.

Avoidance. We keep ourselves busy, always moving forward, as a means of dodging our own feelings. Distraction is a way of avoiding the sometimes uncomfortable process of doing the deep, inner work of the soul.

Guilt. If we slow down while others keep up the pace, we feel guilty. Furthermore, if others depend on our get-stuff-done pace, we don't want to let anybody down by switching gears.

Which of those five rings truest for you? Circle one (or more). Feel free to add additional reasons here.

Deep inside, we know we ought to slow down. But even the word *slow* can have a negative connotation. On the lines below, write a few negative words that come to mind when you think of the word *slow*.

The word *slow* originates from the Old English *slaw*, which means "inactive, sluggish, torpid, lazy." In addition, the Proto-Germanic meaning is "not clever." Other early meanings are blunt, dull, tedious, lethargic.[2]

No wonder *slow* gets a bad rap. Just think if I had named this Bible study the *Growing Lethargic Bible Study* or the *Growing Sluggish Bible*

Study! This is called the *Growing Slow Bible Study*, but you didn't pick up this Bible study because you were looking for the five secrets to lazy living. When you saw the words *Growing Slow*, your heart craved something beautiful, something sacred, something that you almost forgot was possible in this rushed world we live in.

Yes, there are negative connotations to the word *slow*, but there are also many positive ones. Take a moment to ponder the enticing invitation of the word *slow*. What does a slower way of living offer you?

We all want that, don't we? To enjoy the simple moments, to really breathe and feel the air filling our lungs. To connect more deeply with our people. To give loved ones more eye contact and our full attention. To actually *taste* the food we eat, to notice the color of the sky, to embrace the magical nows, and to stop treating life like an emergency.

We think it takes strength and courage to rush through life. But real courage comes in slowing down. Let's stop rushing things that need time to grow—including us.

LET'S STOP RUSHING THINGS THAT NEED TIME TO GROW.

HOLY LAND

God must care deeply about growth. And to make his point, in Scripture he repeatedly calls us to pay attention to our natural world: vines needing pruning, wheat being gleaned, soil being planted.

Let's go back to one of the most popular planting stories of all time, told by one of the greatest storytellers of all time: Jesus. In one parable, Jesus uses seed and soil to teach an important lesson about what God wants to grow within us. Imagine yourself in the crowd, at the edge of a lake, as Jesus tells his story from a boat, just offshore.

The story is told in Matthew, Mark, and Luke. Today we'll focus mostly on Mark's retelling. Read Mark 4:1–9, and then fill in the chart with brief answers.

	Mark 4:4	Mark 4:5–6	Mark 4:7	Mark 4:8
Where did the seeds fall?				
What happened to the seed?				

Perhaps you are scratching your heads, wondering, *What in the world does this have to do with me?* You're not alone. After Jesus and his disciples left the lake, they asked him about the parable (see Mark 4:10).

Jesus graciously spells it out for us.

Read Luke 8:11. Fill in the blanks.

The seed is _____ _____ _____ _____.

Now let's dig in deeper to see what this means for each of us. Read Mark 4:14–20, and then fill in the chart.

	Path Mark 4:15	Rocky Mark 4:16–17	Thorny Mark 4:18–19	Good Mark 4:20
What does Jesus say was the meaning of this type of soil?				
Has your heart ever been like this soil? If so, how?				

I used to think that the first three types of soil—the soil on the path, in the rocks, and in the thorns—applied only to unbelieving people who just didn't "get it." *Poor lost souls! If only they would open their hearts to God's Word!* But then I took a good look at my heart, and can I be honest with you? I didn't like what I saw. I have four chambers in my heart—and that's the right number to hold all four types of soil. I have been shallow, thorny, rebellious, sinful. There's more. I've been selfish, disillusioned, insecure, unkind, disobedient, and fickle.

With all of my four-chambered heart, I want to be a Good Soil Girl 100 percent of the time. But I have come to terms with the fact that I've been as hard-hearted as a slab of concrete.

Many obstacles get in the way of God's seeds growing in our lives. I'll bet most of us can relate to the thorny soil in particular. Let's take a closer look.

Read Mark 4:18–19. Note the three things that choke out the word like thorns do.

This I know for sure: a God-fearing, Bible-believing, sold-out-for-Jesus girl can desire to follow the Lord with all her heart and still find herself overwhelmed by "the worries of this life, the deceitfulness of wealth and the desires for other things."

How have each of those three thorns made themselves evident in your life? Circle the one that has tripped you up the most, and then in the space provided, take note of how any (or all) of these thorns have been an issue for you.

Thorn #1: The Worries of This Life
Thorn #2: The Deceitfulness of Wealth
Thorn #3: The Desires for Other Things

Ouch. Those thorns hurt. They convict. I know all too well the discomfort of conviction. We both got a healthy bit of conviction in session 1, when we invited God to cultivate, or turn over, the soil of our hearts so we could come face-to-face with the sins that trip us up in our journey of growth. It's possible that you feel a little convicted right now as well, as we consider the soil of our hearts.

But don't let the enemy take a healthy bit of conviction and twist that into condemnation.

Conviction comes from the Holy Spirit. Condemnation (and its first cousin shame) come from the enemy.

Condemnation tries to keep you where you are, telling you you'll never be enough.

Conviction says there's a way forward.

The essence of the gospel is that Jesus took all of our sins, our infirmities, our wrongs, our mistakes, our rebellion. He took up every one of the thorns in our soil, even letting them cut his brow.

Read Matthew 27:28–29. Fill in the blanks.

> They stripped him and put a scarlet robe on him, and then twisted together
> a _____ _____ _____ and set it on his head.

Pause for a moment to take in the lengths that Jesus went to in order demonstrate his love for us, even when we were hard-hearted, thorny, rebellious, and sinful. This is our overwhelming, selfless, never-give-up-on-us Savior.

In *Growing Slow* (page 35), I recall how God keeps planting seeds in me even when my soil is thorny and prickly.

> God won't stop planting in you, either.
> Do you see how hopelessly in love with us he is? We are so much more than our shallow, stubborn, disillusioned, insecure, or prickly selves. We

are fields that a divine Farmer refuses to give up on! Let's not confuse the state of our soil with the mysterious, unrelenting affection of a God who loves to watch us grow.

This is unconditional love and acceptance—that God keeps planting.

Jesus is in the business of redeeming all things. He makes beauty from ashes. Turns darkness into light. Brings life from death. And makes crowns from thorns.

But let's not mistake that crown for a symbol of defeat.

Our crowned Savior, King Jesus, reigns.

The twenty-four elders fall down before him who sits on the throne and worship him who lives for ever and ever. They lay their crowns before the throne and say:

> "You are worthy, our Lord and God,
>   to receive glory and honor and power,
> for you created all things,
>   and by your will they were created
>   and have their being."
>
> Revelation 4:10–11

UN-HURRY YOUR HEART

Let's review some key points from this session as we get ready to apply the lessons to our lives.

- Even as we are planting good seeds in the fields God has assigned to us, we ourselves are also being planted.
- We need to stop rushing things that need time to grow.
- We are slow grown by God.

- God loves us even when our hearts are hard, thorny, selfish, and sinful, but in order to grow, we need to come to terms with those parts of our hearts and repent.

Of the points mentioned, circle the one that means the most to you in this season of your life.

I don't want us to miss how each one of those points profoundly impacts our quality of life. There is so much at stake. If we don't slow down, we'll miss the beauty of invaluable gifts from God. We'll be blinded to the sacred act of God planting seeds within us.

You likely sense that God is calling you to a slower way, or you wouldn't have picked up this Bible study. What holds you back?

Perhaps you jotted a few notes related to the Five Reasons We Hurry on pages 38–39. Or maybe you feel like slowing down is impossible with all that's going on. You may feel like you have no choice but to multitask, to drive ten miles over the speed limit, to eat on the run, and to answer emails in the Target checkout line.

Here's some really great news. Multiple experts will tell you that the fastest way to productivity . . . *is to actually slow down*. Growing Slow is your new superpower!

Some of the benefits of slowing down: You'll avoid making mistakes, think more rationally, and have better focus.[3] When you come to a full stop every now and then, you'll give your mind space it needs to become more creative and better at problem-solving.[4]

That doesn't mean you have to stop doing all the things you're tasked to do. It *does* mean you can do them slowly and deliberately, taking deep breaths and breaks in between.

I offer a few ideas on page 11 of *Growing Slow*.

We don't need to complicate this. It's the simple things that will pull us out of the culture of hurry:

Refusing to multitask, instead focusing on the single task before you.

Lighting candles at the dinner table, so you can linger with your family.

Sitting down while you eat, so you can taste the food.

Resisting the urge to check your phone at the stoplight.

Looking in their eyes—really looking—when they tell you a story.

Taking time to celebrate accomplishments, instead of flinging yourself forward to the next thing.

Circle at least one of the six ideas above and commit to trying it in the coming week. When you do, pay attention to how simple, small acts can un-hurry your heart.

This is the way of our Lord—slow, steady, un-hurried. Just as he led the Israelites to the promised land, he is leading you to yours. There's a fascinating story in Scripture that should give us hope and comfort when we don't instantaneously see results as we move toward our promised land.

In the story, the Israelites have been delivered from slavery. They are in the wilderness on their way to the promised land. God explained to them how he would drive out the Hivites, Canaanites, Hittities, and others to make way for the Israelites to claim their promised land.

Read Exodus 23:29–30, and then fill in the blanks.

I will not drive them out in a single year, because the land would become desolate and the wild animals too numerous for you. _____
_____ I will drive them out before you, until you have increased enough to take possession of the land.

God could have given them the land all at once. But he knew a better way: little by little.

In the verses above, underline the apparent consequence of giving over the land all at once.

Sometimes, God chooses slowness because he wants to build patience with his children. Other times, he slows us down to protect us. "Little by little" is how God chooses to roll sometimes. And that might be for our own good.

You are likely eager to jump into your promised land right now. You may feel impatient. But get a little quiet. Go a little slow. Pay attention to this season you're in. God knows what he's doing. He's moving you forward, little by little.

You are a seed planter, and God promises that the growth will come.

Read Psalm 92:12–14 below. Underline the word *will* every time you see it.

The righteous will flourish like a palm tree,
    they will grow like a cedar of Lebanon;
planted in the house of the LORD,
    they will flourish in the courts of our God.
They will still bear fruit in old age,
    they will stay fresh and green.

You *will* flourish. Your seeds *will* flourish. Maybe you'll see great growth tomorrow. Maybe you'll see it happen little by little. But you will see growth.

You will.

PRAYER

Take a deep breath, seed planter. Feel the relief that comes from knowing that God will grow your seeds, little by little. We can enjoy life so much more when we trust God with our endeavors. We can plant our seeds without checking their progress hour by hour. We can step away and take the time to enjoy the little things in life—the taste of a fresh strawberry, the scent of a lilac, the softness of a toddler's cheek, the color of a rainbow after a storm, the embrace of an old friend. Let's pray that God gives us the courage to grow slow.

Dear Lord,

Your Word says good things will grow from these seeds—not might grow, but will grow. Help me believe that it's true. Thank you, Lord, for rummaging around in the soil of my heart to plant seeds. Thank you for never giving up on me, even when I've been hard-hearted, selfish, unyielding, and thorny. Today, I especially thank you for this:

....

....

....

....

In Jesus' name, amen.

GROW

HOW TO FLOURISH UNDER PRESSURE

"I am the vine; you are the branches. If you remain in me and I in you, you will bear much fruit; apart from me you can do nothing."

John 15:5

WEEK 3 FOCUS

- to recognize that beautiful growth can happen in the most unexpected fields
- to see how God can bring purpose from pain

LET'S GET STARTED

Read chapters 7 and 9 of *Growing Slow*. (Optional: chapters 8 and 10.)

Watch a free teaching video from Jennifer based on this week's session. Visit www.GrowingSlowBook.com/Resources to find the video. When prompted, enter this code for access: JDLGrowingSlow.

Last week, we gained a fresh understanding of how God is planting seeds in each of us, his fields. We learned that God often chooses slow growth, moving us forward little by little as he did with the Israelites when he gave over the land little by little.

This week, we will jump right into our fields, paying special attention to the growth that is emerging at this very moment. Can you see it? Sometimes we are in such a rush that we miss the miracle of a seed bursting forth from the ground. Other times we see the growth, but when we compare our fields to someone else's, we minimize the value of the small, good things we are growing.

Around here, on hot summer Sundays, farmers take slow drives in their pickup trucks to examine the crops. We can do the same thing. Buckle up, and let's take a drive.

In this exercise, you will consider the things God is growing *in* you (such as patience, humility, obedience, etc.). Also, you will consider the things God is growing *through* you (your business, ministry, relationships, etc.).

The growth IN you: **In general, how do you feel when you consider what God has been growing in the field of your soul these days? Circle all the words that apply.**

satisfied

restless

disappointed

impatient

grateful

peaceful

weary

flourishing

Name one area where you can see growth happening *in* you. It doesn't have to be huge growth. Even small growth deserves celebrating.

The growth THROUGH you: In general, how do you feel when you consider what God has been growing *through* you? Circle all the words that apply.

satisfied

restless

disappointed

impatient

grateful

peaceful

weary

flourishing

Name one area where you see growth happening *through* you. Again, it doesn't have to be huge growth. Little shoots of green in our fields are worthy of mention, too!

Doesn't that feel good to celebrate the good growth God is doing in you and through you? Hold on to that truth, for it will sustain you, especially in seasons when growth seems like an impossibility.

Now, let's get growing.

MY LAND

On our farm, we pray for ideal conditions: rain at the right time, the heat of the sun, fertile soil, and more. But ideal conditions are, well, idealistic. I can hardly think of a year when everything went as planned. I remember years of drought, hailstorms, flooded fields. Even then, growth eventually happened.

Growth can happen in the most unexpected places and in the most undesirable conditions. Every year, I marvel at how the most beautiful wild mustard plants push up through the pebbles on our country lane.

With enough determination, a beautiful thing can grow anywhere. That's a sweet image—a plant bursting forth from rocky soil.

But what about us? Can we grow in hard places, too?

My godmother's life suggests that we can. Janet was a beautiful soul who grew in the soil of adversity. Janet had multiple health problems all of her adult life. Yet she had an uncanny ability to see and serve people who were themselves suffering and hurting. I always thought that God gave her special eyes. Looking back, I think that one of the reasons she could see the hurt in other people is because she had suffered so much herself. No one would have faulted her if she had become bitter or closed off from time to time. She could have been so consumed by her suffering that she became blinded to the suffering of others.

But instead of her pain becoming a blindfold, it was a magnifying glass. Janet always *saw* the hurting because she *was* the hurting.

I often wonder if Janet's own pain became fuel for her most passionate prayers, the reason she reached out to the rest of us in our own suffering.

Writer Frederick Buechner had a name for this. He called it the "stewardship of pain."

Keep in touch with your pain, Buechner advised:

Keep in touch with it because it is at those moments of pain where you are most open to the pain of other people—most open to your own deep places. Keep in touch with those sad times, those painful times, because it is then that you are most aware of two things—your own powerlessness, crushed in a way by what is happening to you, but also most aware of God's power to somehow pull you through it, to be with you in it.[1]

Observing Janet's life, this becomes clear: Personal pain can be a potent seed.

A few days before she died, I visited her at the hospital. She was frail but wide-eyed. And she was smiling, the kind of smile that came from the inside. I bent over the rail of her bed, and our faces were so close that I could feel her breath on my cheek, like a small, warm fog coasting in and out of her. Though clumsy with grief, I fought for words to express my love.

It pained me to say good-bye, though she was thoroughly ready to meet Jesus. Her eyes were thick with faith, the way they always were. And her body was tired, the way it always was.

I told her how much I loved her. I told her how big of a difference she made, even in her suffering. The hands of affliction seemed to tighten their grip on her in the final years of life. But that only seemed to strengthen her grip on Jesus. She was like a wounded healer, bringing love to the hurting, even in her dying.

Up until the very end, she poured out her love on people—a steward of her pain. It was not we who comforted her. It was she who comforted us. When I leaned over my godmother's bed while tears tore paths down my cheeks, she looked at me with eyes that knew both heartache and healing. She spoke words of comfort and lifted a hand to wipe my tears.

At times, it's difficult for me to see how growing in times of hardship or suffering is even possible. Except that I've seen it happen—in people like Janet.

Good things can grow in the soil of adversity.

GOOD THINGS CAN GROW IN THE SOIL OF ADVERSITY.

YOUR LAND

Perhaps you have a Janet in your life, who has grown in the soil of adversity. Write his or her name below. (Bonus activity: If your "Janet" is still living, consider writing him or her a note of encouragement.)

When I consider some of the most successful people I know, I am amazed at how they didn't wait for ideal conditions in which to grow. When I say "successful," I am not talking only about CEOs and Instagram influencers with a million followers. I am mostly talking about ordinary, everyday people who stewarded what they were given—their gifts, their talents, and even their pain.

I think of a friend who has lost several babies to miscarriage. She started a ministry for moms experiencing pregnancy loss. I think of a recovering alcoholic in our church who spends countless hours mentoring other recovering alcoholics.

Who else but a cancer survivor understands the terrain of the chemo journey? Who else but a recovering addict can better help an addict? If you've lost a child, gone bankrupt, walked through a divorce . . . you are an expert in knowing what it takes to put one foot in front of the other.

The very thing that has caused you the most hurt might be the thing God wants to repurpose for moments of greatest growth.

THE VERY THING THAT HAS CAUSED YOU THE MOST HURT MIGHT BE THE THING GOD WANTS TO REPURPOSE FOR MOMENTS OF GREATEST GROWTH.

Think of a time when you have experienced growth in the soil of adversity. Write about it here.

If you're like me, you pray for ideal conditions to experience abundant growth in your family, career, and spiritual journey. For a farmer, ideal conditions involve the right amount of rain and the perfect amount of sun. Flooding, drought, hail, and pests get in the way of our ideals.

Here's a list of less-than-ideal conditions that keep us from believing that good things can grow through us:

not enough time

not enough influence

health problems

financial constraints

fear of rejection

people-pleasing tendencies

feelings of "not enough"

lack of discipline

lack of consistency

personal suffering

unsupportive friends/family

bad habits

trauma

lack of patience

shortage of confidence

other _____

Circle all that apply to you.

It's painful to be held back by those less-than-ideal conditions. Maybe right now it's all too much. Maybe the suffering is too fresh. Maybe the setbacks you've faced prevent the growth you desire. But I believe there will come a time when we will each stand at a crossroads and have to make the decision to trust that God can grow good things, even in moments of drought and despair. A few famous examples:

Albert Einstein, a Nobel Prize–winning physicist, couldn't get a job in physics for a couple of years after his graduation.

Frederick Douglass was born into slavery and separated from his family, but he became a national leader of the abolitionist movement.

Surfer Bethany Hamilton lost her arm in a shark attack but went on to become a champion surfer.

But let's not forget the ordinary people who take tiny faithful steps every day, sometimes in obscurity, to serve in ministry, raise children, or earn a degree. It's fair to say that every single one of them has faced adversity, too. How can I be so sure?

Read the words of Jesus in John 16:33. Fill in the blank.

"In this world you _____ have trouble."

In this world you *will* have trouble. Period.

All on its own, that sentence—with its certainty of hardship—would be enough to deflate anyone's hopes for sustainable growth. But Jesus doesn't end his remarks when you get to that period, right after the word *trouble*. There's a promise that comes after the period:

"In this world you will have trouble. But take heart! I have overcome the world."

In this world you will have trouble. *Period.*

Then comes the *promise*: Jesus has overcome the world.

But wait! There's more. Let's not miss those three little words between the period and the promise. **Circle those three words in the verse above.**

The truth is, most of us are living in between the period and the promise. We have experienced trouble. Period. But until heaven, we won't get to experience the fullness of Jesus' promise that he has "overcome the world."

Until then, let's "take heart."

Jesus didn't say that we should "take control." He didn't say we should "take matters into our own hands." He didn't say we should "take a pass."

He calls us to take heart. Exclamation point!

Where are you living between the period and the promise, and need Jesus' encouragement to "take heart"?

HOLY LAND

Today's trip through the Holy Land will take us on quite a journey. We'll visit a pit, a prison, and a palace.

Our tour guide: Joseph.

In writing the book of Genesis, Moses spent considerable time focused on Joseph and his journey through the land. We could spend this whole Bible study gleaning important lessons from Joseph. If you want to read the entire story, take some time to dig into Genesis 37:1 through 50:26. In this week's session, we'll focus on a few of the highlights.

Read Genesis 37:1–10. Record anything you learned about the following:

The land* where Joseph lived: _____

Joseph's age: _____

Joseph's relationship with his dad:

*Fun fact: Remember the Hebrew word *eretz* that we studied in session 1? That's the word used here.

60

Joseph's relationship with his brothers:

The drama is about to heighten as Joseph's brothers contend with their jealousy and anger. The brothers hit the road to graze their dad's flocks. They go to Shechem first, and then to Dothan. Joseph doesn't come until later, and when they see him approaching Dothan, they cook up a plan.

Read Genesis 37:16–18. What did the brothers plan to do to the favored son, Joseph?

The plot thickens.

Read Genesis 37:19–20. Where did the brothers throw their brother?

Read Genesis 37:21–28 and verse 36. Briefly summarize Joseph's next step of the journey.

Poor Joseph. Left in a pit. Sold off by his brothers. Carted away to Egypt. It's hard to imagine what good could come from this soil of adversity that Joseph has been planted in.

Read Genesis 39:1–5. In this time of great transition in Joseph's life, who was his steady companion? Fill in the blanks from verse 2.

_____ _____ was with Joseph so that he prospered.

This story gives me hope, but it also gives me pause. I have hope, because it shows me that the Lord sticks to us like Velcro, even when we are dwelling in a pit. He can bring great growth in strange ways and places. Joseph "prospered"!

But it also gives me pause, because current seasons of prosperity don't shield us from future seasons of pain and suffering.

Read Genesis 39:6–20. Where did Joseph end up?

The story looks bleak at this point. Prisons in Joseph's day were "grim places with vile conditions. They were used to house forced laborers or, like Joseph, the accused who were awaiting trial. Prisoners were guilty until proven innocent, and there was no right to a speedy trial. Many prisoners never made it to court, because trials were held at the whim of the ruler."[2]

If ever Joseph needed a Velcro-type Lord to stick close, it was then. And that's exactly what he got.

Read Genesis 39:21. Fill in the blanks.

_____ was with him; he showed him kindness and granted him favor in the eyes of the prison warden.

In the next few verses (22–24), note that Joseph is put in charge of many tasks. Joseph takes each task—big or small—and gives it his all. From last session, you'll recall that God likes to grow us little by little. We are slow grown—even Joseph, who found himself Growing Slow in the soil of adversity.

The next part of Joseph's story suggests that time wore on . . . and on . . . and on for him.

His story, unfolding in Genesis 40, uses terminology like "some time later" (verse 1) and "after they had been in custody for some time" (verse 4).

And then, Joseph's big break finally comes.

> When two full years had passed, Pharaoh had a dream.
>
> Genesis 41:1

In the verse above, underline the passage of time.

Because Joseph has earned a reputation in prison as a dream interpreter, he is called on to interpret Pharaoh's dream. And, with God's help, Joseph spells it all out.

His reward?

> Then Pharaoh said to Joseph, "Since God has made all this known to you, there is no one so discerning and wise as you. You shall be in charge of my palace, and all my people are to submit to your orders."
>
> Genesis 41:39–40

How old was Joseph at the time when he was put in charge of Egypt? Read Genesis 41:46 and write the answer here:

Remember how old Joseph was at the beginning of this story? He was barely a man. Thirteen years passed. And in those years, Joseph moved from a pit to a prison to a palace. That's a remarkable testimony of growth—slow, steady, hard growth.

Don't hear me saying we are all going to end up living in castles with fat bank accounts thirteen years from now. I don't subscribe to a "prosperity gospel" that promises financial blessing and success.

What I am saying is this: God can grow something in you—and through you—no matter the season, the circumstance, or the timing.

Right now, you may feel like you are in a prison. Maybe you are in a pit. Maybe you see some proverbial palace in the skyline up ahead. Like he was with Joseph, the Lord is with you as well, right by your side, even when the growing conditions aren't ideal.

When Joseph finally became a father, he named one of his boys Ephraim. Why did he pick that name?

Read Genesis 41:52. Fill in the blanks.

"It is because God has made me _____ _____."

I could just about cry reading those words. It floors me to think that God can make something out of the messes I find myself in, even the messes I make. I might be a hot mess, but Jesus loves this hot mess, and he is determined to grow something—even when the growing conditions aren't ideal.

I can bear fruit, even in "the land of my suffering."* Let's be good stewards, even of our pain.

UN-HURRY YOUR HEART

As I grow slow, Joseph's story gives me hope. How about you?

*Once more, "land" here is the Hebrew word *eretz*. I'll never look at that word the same!

In what ways can this knowledge about Joseph help un-hurry your heart today?

Let me confess something to you. When I consider the "land of my suffering" (some translations say "the land of my affliction"), my first prayer isn't, "Oh, dear God, help me to be fruitful in that land!" I want to get *out* of that land!

Yet Scripture paints a clear picture that sustainable growth happens in the midst of difficulty. In fact, Jesus said in John 12:24 that "a single grain of wheat doesn't produce anything unless it is planted in the ground *and dies*. If it dies, it will produce a lot of grain" (GW, emphasis added).

I don't want suffering. I don't want the seed in the ground to die. But Jesus said the seed must die. What does that look like for us? I wrote about that on page 43 of *Growing Slow*:

> Our will must die. Our desire to rush through hard seasons must die. Our belief that we're in charge here must die. Our demands. Our misguided plans. Our selfish ambitions. All of it must die.

Underline any of the sentences or phrases above that speak loudest to you. Or is there something else that "must die"? Some sin? Some struggle? If so, write it here:

The cornerstone of the Christian faith is believing that life can come from death. As we close, consider a past or current season of suffering and the growth that came from it.

Name the following:

The land of your suffering or affliction: _____

The seeds that you have (or will) plant in that land:

_____

The growth you are seeing already: _____

The hoped-for harvest: _____

Your field is so beautiful, my friend. Take it all in. Enjoy the view. This is the place God has you, for such a time as this. And now, take a moment to see who's standing next to you, at the edge of your glorious field. Let Joseph's words reach forward to tell you exactly who that is:

The LORD was with Joseph.

> Genesis 39:2

And the Lord is with you.

"Surely I am with you always, to the very end of the age."

> Matthew 28:20

Thanks be to God.

PRAYER

For many years, where I live in rural America, I've seen wall hangings, greeting cards, and plaques with a blessing called the Farmer's Prayer.[3]

Ponder the "farm" where you plant your seeds—whether you live in Manhattan, Missouri, or Maui. Let's pray this simple prayer together as we close:

> Lord, bless the land you've given me,
> And may I always know
> As I tend each crop and creature
> You're the one who helps them grow.
>
> Grant me the strength and wisdom
> Please protect me from harm,
> And thank you
> For your gracious gift—
> The blessing of a farm.

HARVEST

GROW . . . AND MAKE DISCIPLES

"The harvest is plentiful but the workers are few."

Matthew 9:37

WEEK 4 FOCUS

- to gain the courage to be an ambassador of the Good News, right where you are
- to hand over the people you love the most to God's loving care

LET'S GET STARTED

There are no assigned readings for this session. (Optional: Read chapters 12–15 of *Growing Slow*.)

Watch a free teaching video from Jennifer based on this week's session. Visit www.GrowingSlowBook.com/Resources to find the video. When prompted, enter this code for access: JDLGrowingSlow.

For the last several sessions, we focused on what God is growing *in* us and on what God is growing *through* us. Today, we make a vital shift in our Growing Slow journey. Because this journey is not our own. An essential part of the Christian life is to faithfully engage with the people God has placed in our lives—not only in our homes and workplaces, but with the people on the periphery of our lives. They are all there for a reason. And like you, they are all fields being planted by God.

But there's a good chance that God is going to put some of the seeds in our hands. Do we have the courage to plant those seeds? Are we willing to tell people that they are loved by God, that Christ forgives sins, that there's a Father in heaven who hears their cries for help in times of trouble?

> But how can people call for help if they don't know who to trust? And how can they know who to trust if they haven't heard of the One who can be trusted? And how can they hear if nobody tells them? And how is anyone going to tell them, unless someone is sent to do it?
>
> Romans 10:14–15 THE MESSAGE

Yep. We're going there. We are going to talk about evangelism.

In your opinion, what keeps people from sharing the gospel with others?

Mark on the scale below how comfortable you feel sharing the gospel with others.

1 ——————— 2 ——————— 3 ——————— 4 ——————— 5

Not comfortable at all   Very comfortable

The word *evangelizing* can conjure up uncomfortable images of a guy on a street corner with a bullhorn and a sign commanding you to repent before it's too late. And, in recent years, the word *evangelize*—along with its first cousin *evangelical*—has gotten tangled up politically. But let's set politics and negative connotations aside and take a look at the root word in Greek, *eu-angelion. Eu* means "good" and *angelion* means "message."

So in its biblical form, a person who evangelizes would be carrying the "good message" about Jesus.

Friend, this session isn't going to give you guidance on how to be an obnoxious fire-and-brimstone street-corner preacher with a political agenda.

This session is all about sharing the love. It's about living the sermon as much as it is preaching it (but also not being afraid to preach it when God provides the opportunity).

As someone once said, "You may be the only Bible some people ever read."[1]

My hope is that, together, we can uncover a revolutionary and timely path toward sharing Christ with others in meaningful ways with eternal value.

Let's *grow* . . . and make disciples.

MY LAND

Growing up, we lived one block away from the United Methodist Church. On Sundays, I walked there with my dad. In patent-leather shoes, I tried to keep up with his stride, but I had to take two steps for every one of his. My Strawberry Shortcake dress would swing in the morning breeze.

I still remember what my hand felt like in his. You don't forget a thing like that.

Inside the church, Mom sang Bill Gaither Trio gospel songs with a trio of women. Paul Fullenworth was the usher, and a lady named LillyLove sat in the front row—nodding with certainty about the promise of salvation. During the service, I played hangman with my best friend, Carla, and we'd giggle inappropriately during the sermon. During Sunday school, Hortense told us that Jesus loved us no matter what. She taught us how to clasp our hands together and make the church and steeple with our fingers before turning them inside out to "see all the people."

Many Sundays, we'd gather in the basement fellowship hall for potlucks—with thick-sauced lasagna, bowls of fruit suspended in Jell-O, and my godmother Janet's famous egg coffee.

As I look back on my life, I see the faces of so many people who quietly impacted my faith journey. Only a handful had degrees in ministry. But they all planted seeds in me when I was a young "field."

If I could plot my life on a timeline and label it with people and experiences who planted seeds in me, I'd place my gentle-hearted Sunday school teachers Hortense and Rose toward the beginning of my life. I'd include my parents, my godmother, and my oldest sister, who gave me my very first study Bible. I'd include two friends who invited my husband and me to a three-day retreat that profoundly impacted our relationship with the Lord. I'd even include strangers, like Beth Moore, whom I've never met but who guided me through numerous Bible studies.

On my timeline, I wouldn't be able to mark a certain day when I was saved, because my faith journey didn't have a moment of conversion like that. Perhaps yours does. I do know this: From the beginning of time, God called me his own, and he placed seeds in the hands of common, ordinary people who took the time to love me.

YOUR LAND

I am so excited about the creative, meaningful exercise we are going to undertake in this session to remember the people who planted seeds in our hearts. We are going to label a timeline with years. Then, on the timeline, we will plot names of people (or experiences) that drew our hearts closer to Christ. It could be that you are a new Christian, and you didn't have many interactions with believers until recently. That's okay too! Even so, take some time to think back on your life and remember people who influenced you positively. Consider youth leaders, teachers, neighbors, friends, someone you met on a mission trip, bunkmates at Bible camp, a nurse who prayed, even a stranger you encountered who impacted you in an unexpected way. Your story is your story, and these people are not only the seed planters, but the fertilizer needed to help you grow.

At the beginning of the timeline below, place your date of birth. Then divide your life, in years, between the ten segments. Then plot the names of people or moments that impacted you in those periods.

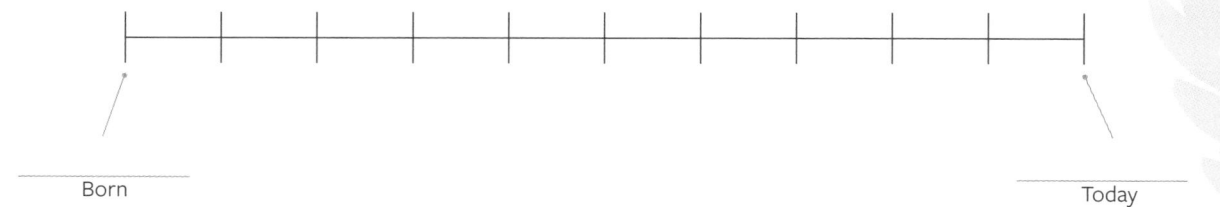

Born

Today

Reflecting on your timeline, what is the main emotion running through you?

After I filled out my timeline, I felt an overwhelming sense of gratitude for the people who went out of their way to demonstrate the gospel to me, in both word and deed. It floors me to think that God knew all along who my seed planters were. And he knew yours, too. He knew the places where you'd live, the characters you'd encounter, and the voices who'd have the most influence on your spiritual growth.

What astounds me most is that the people who have most positively impacted my spiritual journey don't have any kind of ministry training. They were simply people who showed up. They showed up at Sunday school to teach simple songs. They showed up to put a Bible in my little hands. When I grew into adulthood, they showed up when I was suffering from postpartum depression, facing personal struggles, and grieving the loss of loved ones. They showed up in text messages and on my doorstep when I needed a friend.

I am reminded of the seed planters in my life whenever I come across Acts 4:13.

Read Acts 4:13. Fill in the blanks.

When they saw the _____ of Peter and John and realized that they were _____ , _____ men, they were astonished and took note that these men _____ _____ _____ _____.

Do you have any "unschooled, ordinary" seed planters on your timeline? How have their lives displayed evidence that they have "been with Jesus"?

Now it's time to shift the focus from the seed planters in your life and focus on those seeds in your hands. Maybe you are "unschooled" in the ways of sharing Jesus. Even if you *do* have a degree in ministry, perhaps you feel quite "ordinary."

How does the story of Peter and John give you courage today?

In the Un-Hurry Your Heart section of this session, you'll have an opportunity to put that courage into action. But before we get there, let's visit the Holy Land and reacquaint ourselves with some powerful words from God, "the Lord of the harvest."

HOLY LAND

This session's theme verse comes from Matthew 9:37: "The harvest is plentiful but the workers are few."

To study the verse in context, open your Bible and read Matthew 9:35–10:8.

There's so much to unpack. In this story, Jesus had spent considerable time traveling through towns and villages, preaching and healing. Jesus was, in a word, busy. And I thought the demands on *my* life were extensive! At this point, if I were Jesus, I would have been exhausted. I confess that the last thing I would want to do is face another demanding crowd. I would be Googling "all-inclusive spa resorts on Sea of Galilee."

But Jesus didn't take a vacation when he saw the crowds. According to Matthew 9:36, what emotion overcame Jesus? Write it here.

Let's pause and consider the compassion we have for people. Do our attitudes toward those people match up with Jesus' view? Let's start with our families. How about our neighbors? The people who are constantly asking us for something? The woman who cut in line at Chick-fil-A? Our competitors? Our "enemies"?

Jesus was motivated by compassion. He didn't see a crowd full of irritating, annoying people who wanted something. He had compassion on them and saw that they were "harassed and helpless." He recognized their great need for a Savior; he also recognized a tremendous opportunity.

"The harvest is plentiful."

These people in front of him were a field ripe for harvest, ready to hear the *eu-angelion,* "the good message." They were ready, but someone needed to tell them. The problem wasn't a lack of harvestable "crops," so to speak. It was a lack of workers! "The workers are few."

In this apparent labor shortage, Jesus could have given a stirring message worthy of a mic drop. But instead of personally delivering the "good message" on his own, what did Jesus do? Read Matthew 9:38 and write Jesus' directions here:

I find this incredibly interesting. First, Jesus could have done the evangelizing himself. He is the Son of God, after all. Second, he doesn't direct the disciples to go out right away. He directs them to pray first! "Ask the Lord of the harvest. . . ."

I would have imagined that Jesus would have immediately sent out his disciples to do the work of harvest. Time was ticking! But instead, Jesus tells them to pray.

Why do you suppose that is? Write your reflections here.

I wish I could read your answer. I'll share mine. To me, these verses suggest three things:

1. There are more people truly wanting to hear about Jesus than there are people willing to share.
2. Prayer must precede even our most well-meaning actions.
3. We are made to live and serve in community, with co-laborers.

The story continues with Jesus calling twelve of his followers, authorizing them with his power, and then sending them out.

In *The Message,* Eugene Peterson calls these twelve people the "harvest hands" of Christ. These are their instructions:

"Don't begin by traveling to some far-off place to convert unbelievers. And don't try to be dramatic by tackling some public enemy. Go to the lost, confused people right here in the neighborhood. Tell them that the kingdom is here. Bring health to the sick. Raise the dead. Touch the untouchables. Kick out the demons. You have been treated generously, so live generously.

"Don't think you have to put on a fund-raising campaign before you start. You don't need a lot of equipment. *You* are the equipment, and all you need to keep that going is three meals a day. Travel light."

Matthew 10:5–10 THE MESSAGE

I won't presume to know how the Holy Spirit is speaking to you as you read those verses. But I'd bet you a bushelful of harvested Iowa corn that he is, indeed, speaking to you.

Reread that section of Scripture and underline or highlight phrases that speak to you personally.

I find the words and actions of Jesus so reassuring. He is reminding me that I can start in my own community, that I don't need to do big dramatic things. I'm called to show up in everyday ways. The line that is sticking with me right now is this: "You have been treated generously, so live generously." I look back on my timeline and think about the ways that unschooled, ordinary men and women impacted my life. I, indeed, was treated generously, and I want to live generously in return.

I want to live my life in such a way that I would end up on someone's timeline.

UN-HURRY YOUR HEART

So far in this session, we have

- considered our level of comfort in sharing the gospel with others
- remembered with fondness the seed planters who showed us Christ's love, not always with words, but quite often with actions
- heard how Jesus wants us to respond to a plentiful harvest—with compassion and prayer

As a reminder, this section is called Un-Hurry Your Heart. This is where we apply principles to calm our hurried hearts. I know how strange this might sound, but we are going to first explore the *urgency* of the task at hand. I promise we'll get to the un-hurried heart applications in a moment. But first, Jesus has something to say to us.

Read John 4:35. Fill in the blanks.

> "Don't you have a saying, 'It's still four months until harvest'? I tell you, open your eyes and look at the fields! They are _____ _____ _____."

At times, we might excuse ourselves from sharing the gospel because we think certain people "aren't ready" to hear it. Jesus suggests that the harvest is ready. Right now, there are people whom God has prepared, in advance, for you to share his great love. When I read Jesus' words, this feels like an urgent call.

What, if anything, would keep you from sharing the gospel? Check all that apply.

- ☐ time investment required
- ☐ fear of rejection
- ☐ previous efforts failed
- ☐ afraid of what people will think
- ☐ ill-equipped
- ☐ other _____

Let me be straight with you. At one time or another, I've struggled with all of those obstacles. I even lost a close friend who completely rejects the gospel and everything about it, including me as a sold-out believer of Christ.

She thinks I am crazy. (Just now, I remember I'm in good company! Even Jesus' family thought he was "out of his mind." See Mark 3:21.)

Jerry Root, a professor of evangelism at Wheaton College, has a fascinating theory about why we are reluctant to share.

> Perhaps one of the reasons we are so hesitant to tell others about Jesus is that we've forgotten how deeply and unconditionally he loves us. . . . The prerequisite to evangelizing is abiding in God's love. Being more concerned about what others think of us than what Jesus thinks of us—that is, forgetting that he loves us—will freeze us in our tracks.[2]

How might "abiding in God's love" equip you to be bold in your witness?

With this urgency to share the gospel, is it possible to un-hurry our hearts? I believe that the urgency comes in planting the seeds. But then, we rest and wait. Sharing the gospel is a school of patience. We "un-hurry our hearts" when we remember that God is doing the real work—in his way and timing. That's the lesson we learn from one of the greatest seed planters of all time: Paul, along with his co-laborer Apollos.

Read 1 Corinthians 3:6. Who planted? Who watered? And who caused the growth?

My heart feels un-hurried when I remember this: My job is obedience to the call. God's job is results.

I know that many of you are faithful co-laborers in the harvest. If you're like me, it's easy to run ahead of the Lord of the harvest. We want to see the fruit now. But God changes lives over time. Sometimes the fields are ripe for harvest a day after planting; other times, it could take years. This is not a harvest dependent on weather. People aren't corn seeds. They are souls, slow grown and loved by God from beginning to end.

Has the Lord put someone on your heart as you went through this session? Maybe that someone is a loved one who doesn't know Jesus. Maybe that someone is a friend who has fallen away from the faith. Maybe that someone is a longtime follower of Christ who is going through a really rough time. Delivering the *eu-angelion* to people might mean sitting down and presenting the gospel in a straightforward way. But it could mean simply showing up with a Starbucks and a willingness to listen. It could mean inviting the neighbors over for dinner on a Saturday night. (For a compelling example, read Wayne and Kim's story in chapter 11 of *Growing Slow*, "The One Where We Grow Slow with Friends.")

We actually *need* to slow down in order to have such opportunities. Evangelism itself—getting those opportunities to offer hope—often come in those slow moments of life when we take time to really be present with others.

> How beautiful are the feet of those who bring *good news*!
>
> Romans 10:15, emphasis added

There's that word again—*eu-angelion*.

Do you want to share Jesus with the world in the coming week? Simply take those beautiful feet of yours and walk the path with others. Serve. Bow low. Give. Slow down and really *be present* with people. Offer comfort, even at your own discomfort. Love. With simple acts of service, people will see Jesus alive in you. Your life will preach a sermon even when your lips aren't moving.

How beautiful are the feet of friends who drive neighbors to chemo.

How beautiful are the feet of foster mothers who won't stop praying for God's unstoppable love to break through.

How beautiful are the feet of nursing-home workers who care for our elderly brothers and sisters.

How beautiful are the feet of teachers getting classrooms ready for new students while praying over every desk.

How beautiful are the feet of CEOs who bring the ethic of Christ into the workplace.

How beautiful are the feet of poets and songwriters who string together gospel-laced words that help us make sense of the world.

How beautiful are the feet of women everywhere who, in this moment, feel invisible and unseen in their daily tasks, but press on because this is what God called them to.

How beautiful are the feet of those who grow slow and take the time to truly be present with people.

What you are doing matters a great deal, friend. Oh, how beautiful are your feet! It doesn't matter where those feet have been in the past; what matters is where they're going today.

The harvest is plentiful. Take off your shoes and step into the field.

THE HARVEST IS PLENTIFUL. TAKE OFF YOUR SHOES AND STEP INTO THE FIELD.

Who can you reach out to this week? How will you bring the "good message" to their heart?

PRAYER

As we close in prayer, I want to share a story from 2 Kings 7. I read it for the first time many years ago, in the brand-new Bible that my sister gave me. I was so taken by the story that, for the first time in my life, I highlighted a passage in my Bible. The story is about four men with leprosy who were desperate for food during a famine. They decided to raid an enemy army's camp—a risky move indeed, but their hunger spoke louder than their fear.

At dusk they went to the camp, and—surprise!—not a soul was there. The camp had been deserted, but these men hit the jackpot: food, clothing, and gold were in abundance. The men went from tent to tent, eating and drinking and carting away plunder. It was a miracle: Four hungry beggars suddenly found themselves at the feast!

Here's where the story gets really good. Those men turned to each other and said, "What we're doing is not right. This is a day of good news and we are keeping it to ourselves" (2 Kings 7:9).

Friend, this is us.

You are I are a couple of hungry beggars who know where the feast is. It's too good to keep to ourselves.

Dear Lord,

I have been invited to the feast. I have been filled. I have received the "good message" of Christ. I am not a hero. I'm just a hungry beggar who knows where the Feast is. And I see that you have set extra places at the table. Give me the courage to invite some special people in my life to the table. Today, I pray for . . .

_____

_____

_____

In Jesus' name, amen.

CELEBRATE

LET'S GET THIS PARTY STARTED

There, in the presence of the LORD your God, you and your families shall eat and shall rejoice in everything you have put your hand to, because the LORD your God has blessed you.

Deuteronomy 12:7

WEEK 5 FOCUS

- to recover the lost art of celebration
- to give thanks to God for good things, grown slow

LET'S GET STARTED

Read chapters 16, 18, and 19 of *Growing Slow.*

Watch a free teaching video from Jennifer based on this week's session. Visit www.GrowingSlowBook.com/Resources to find the video. When prompted, enter this code for access: JDLGrowingSlow.

On our journey together through God's Word and his land, we have passed through the spring season of cultivating and planting (sessions 1 and 2), the summer season of growth (session 3), and the autumnal season of harvest (session 4).

And then comes winter. Depending on where you live, winter possibly feels empty, barren, and devoid of light and growth. Where I live, winter days can become unspeakably cold. Many retired people in our region fly south for the winter and stay away for months at a time. Even metaphorically, we speak of winter with a sort of bitterness and disdain. Have you ever heard the descriptive phrase "winter of the soul"? It certainly doesn't convey warm, fuzzy feelings, does it?

What positive and negative words or images come to mind as you ponder literal or figurative seasons of winter? I've listed a few to get you started.

NEGATIVE	POSITIVE
lack of growth	beautiful snow
depressing	cozy nights by the fire

Do you tend to view winter favorably or unfavorably?

In my own Growing Slow journey, I came to the realization that I have underestimated the value of winter and the gifts that those seasons of my life have brought me. I wrote on page 171 of *Growing Slow*, "What if winter isn't a season to be escaped, and instead, one to be embraced?"

WHAT IF WINTER ISN'T A SEASON TO BE ESCAPED, AND, INSTEAD, ONE TO BE EMBRACED?

Read the following passage from pages 172–173 of *Growing Slow*, and underline any passages that ring true for you.

Looking back, I can see that the winter seasons of my life grew me in ways I didn't know I needed at the time. They grew faith inside of me that I never imagined possible. In my heart's coldest winters, I learned about perseverance, patience, and endurance, traits that would serve me well in the summers of my heart.

During the winter seasons of life, it appeared as though nothing was happening, and that nothing I did mattered.

There were years of exhaustion, seasons of loneliness, long hospital stays, emergencies, funerals, financial strain, disappointments in ministry, and so much more. I struggled with a dark night of the soul during a long stretch of my early adulthood. In those years, I lost all belief, not only in Jesus' love for me, but in his very existence. . . .

God didn't always move the mountain, but day by day, he provided me with enough grace to climb it. Strength for today; hope for tomorrow. Each day, I added to the muscle and spiritual insight that I would not have gained any other way.

Winter seasons of the heart can reveal themselves not only in times of great trial but in the mundane moments of life.

Can winter, as a season of the heart, be embraced? If so, how?

For the final two sessions of this study, we will mine the season of winter for its hidden treasures. Today, we will explore the gifts of celebration and gratitude.

MY LAND

On our farm, the slowest season of all comes just after the harvest, when fall turns to winter, and it feels natural to give thanks to God in that season of slowing down. We think of thanksgiving as an autumnal celebration, which of course it is. But what if we began to carry such robust, celebratory gratitude throughout our year? What about making it a prominent fixture of the winter seasons of life?

Our church has an annual celebration of thanks called Takk for Alt, harkening to our congregation's Norwegian roots. *Takk for Alt* is Norwegian for "Thanks for everything." For decades our church has celebrated the annual tradition with a Sunday meal in the fellowship hall.

The celebration brings great joy to my heart every year, but it also deeply convicts me about the way my practice of gratitude is emaciated in winter. And I don't mean just the *actual* winter, but primarily the winter of my heart, when life seems barren or sad.

The Bible says to "give thanks in all circumstances; for this is God's will for you in Christ Jesus" (1 Thessalonians 5:18).

Giving thanks in all circumstances and all seasons challenges me. But there it is. We are to be thankful in *all* things. Not just the summer things and the growing things and the wished-for things. But the winter things and the slow things and the hard things. We are instructed to be thankful in times of grief and death and pain and sorrow, those moments that make us wonder if we can stand another day. How to be thankful like *that*? Is it really possible for a mortal to be thankful *in all things*?

Perhaps the answer lies in the preposition. Paul instructed us to be thankful *in* all things; he didn't say to be thankful *for* all things.

During a recent Takk for Alt dinner, we ate our catered meal. Around the fellowship hall, I mentally catalogued my gratitude. That's the easy part of Takk for Alt. There were many blessings to count. I watched how people leaned into one another, laughing. Someone said they'd been praying for my daughter, a kindness that brought me to tears. I smiled, watching two friends—like real sisters—sharing one piece of dessert. This is the sort of thing you do at family tables. And I was thankful that we were like family.

But what about the other, harder half of Takk for Alt? When we say we give thanks, do we really mean we give thanks only in the good times?

After the tables were cleared, we headed over to the sanctuary for our annual business meeting. We discussed several new mission projects, and that was exciting. Again, more easy thanksgiving. But it wasn't until the meeting was nearly adjourned that we saw the fullness of Takk for Alt. It wasn't planned. It just . . . happened.

Before the meeting adjourned, a woman in the back row stood up. Her wobbly voice rose above our small crowd: "I want to tell you how much it meant to me . . ."—she paused, hands gripping the back of a pew in front of her—"when you gave us a 'love gift' of money after the fire. And how you've welcomed us here."

And so began a series of spontaneous praises, thank offerings in the hardest things—proof that we can give thanks *in* all things.

An elderly couple stood up next, expressing thanks to God even though they, too, had watched as a fire destroyed buildings on their farm, flames coming within inches of their house. Much was lost, but they were grateful for what was spared. Another woman stood up, giving thanks for the people who had comforted her in her time of mourning. And on and on it went, people expressing Takk for Alt, not from the mountaintop, but from deep in the valley.

These are the life-changing truths that came into clear focus that day:

- I don't have to wait for perfect conditions to express my gratitude to God.
- It is a gift to celebrate *in community*, together calling out the good things that God is growing in us.
- Winter seasons of life offer built-in pauses for us, giving us time and space to reflect, remember . . . and celebrate.

YOUR LAND

Let's take a moment to consider what gratitude and celebration look like in your life.

How do you make time to express gratitude? If this isn't a regular practice for you, what are the biggest obstacles?

Are there certain seasons when you find yourself most able to express gratitude?

Is it easier to express gratitude during hard times, or during flourishing times?

Reread 1 Thessalonians 5:18: "Give thanks in all circumstances; for this is God's will for you in Christ Jesus." How do those words sit with you today?

In the pages ahead, we will learn that celebration is one of the highest forms of gratitude. We'll study how God instructed the Israelites to carry out certain festivals, feasts, and celebrations, and then how those traditions became an important part of the early church and even the spread of Christianity.

Imagine it! You can be a "party girl" for the gospel.

How does that last sentence strike you right now? Circle the sentence below that most fits your reaction.

Say *what*?

Ooo! I'm intrigued.

Jennifer has lost her ever-lovin' mind.

That sounds sinful.

Let's get this party started!

HOLY LAND

The Bible is the ultimate party guide. To be sure, the Bible is a book filled with stories of great sacrifice, heartbreaking lament, and betrayal. But it's also filled with so much fun and laughter that my heart overflows with joy. The Bible is a book of feasts, festivals, parties, dancing, singing, and celebrating. There are rich foods and fine wines and music.

To get us started, I've listed a handful of the celebratory moments in the Bible.

Read each one, and then jot a response. You can write a just-the-facts response about what took place, or go a step further and imagine the scene. Take note of any emotions that rise up within you.

2 Samuel 6:12–19

Nehemiah 12:27–43

Luke 2:8–14

Luke 2:20

Luke 15:20–24

What other biblical celebrations come to mind for you? I think of the wedding supper of the lamb (Revelation 19), Jesus' making breakfast on the beach for his disciples (John 21), along with imagery from the Psalms and the book of Isaiah.

Read Isaiah 25:6 and fill in the blanks.

On this mountain the _____ _____ will prepare a
_____ of rich food for all peoples, a _____ of aged
wine—the best of meats and the finest of wines.*

What a marvelous prophecy. Reread the words from Isaiah once more. Take special note of *who* is doing the banquet preparation here! God didn't hire a caterer to handle the details. It blows me away to think about the Creator of the universe loving us in such a thoughtful, generous way. He cares so deeply about celebration that he prepares the most exquisite banquet, treating us, his children, as honored guests.

God embraces celebration. But do we?

In our modern age, we've lost the art of celebration. Consider the following:

- Mealtimes are often rushed and hurried rather than savored.
- While we might take time to observe certain holidays, such as Christmas, we are frustrated that the meaning gets lost in commercialism.
- We move past celebrating an accomplishment at work because we see the work still needing to be done.
- Church celebrations can feel rushed or ritualistic. Charles Spurgeon once said, "The Lord's own Supper is a joyful festival, a feast."[1] Yet we've reduced this feast to tiny wafers and a bit of grape juice or wine, taken swiftly so the service doesn't run too long. I wonder what we're missing out on by not taking the time to savor, celebrate, and express our gratitude more thoughtfully.

*The Bible mentions wine a number of times in the context of celebration. Clearly, God does not approve of alcohol abuse, and this session is not intended to promote overdrinking or to encourage anyone who struggles with addiction to drink alcohol. Randy Alcorn, in chapter 33 of his book *Happiness* (Tyndale, 2015), takes a deep dive into biblical celebration and was a tremendously helpful resource for me during research for this session of the Bible study.

In the Old Testament, celebrations were built into the calendar. A key aspect of these festivals: thanksgiving and remembrance.

Let's take a look at three key festivals and consider what they mean for us as Christians today.

Read the following verses and fill in the blanks.

Deuteronomy 16:1–8
Name of festival: _____ *
Reason for celebrating: _____
Key point (from verse 3): "So that all the days of your life you may
_____ _____ _____ of your departure from Egypt."

Deuteronomy 16:9–12
Name of festival: _____ _____ _____
Reason for celebrating: _____
Key point (from verse 11): "And _____ before the LORD your
      God."

Deuteronomy 16:13–15
Name of festival: _____ _____ _____ _____
Reason for celebrating (see also Leviticus 23:42–43 for help answering this question): _____
Key point (from verse 15): "For the LORD your God will _____
_____ in all your harvest and in all the work of your hands,
and _____ _____ _____ _____ _____."

Notice the themes of thanksgiving, expressed joy, and remembrance of God's protection.

*Also called the Festival of Unleavened Bread (see Deuteronomy 16:16).

Like the Israelites, we need rituals and celebrations to help us remember, to renew our faith, and to create a lasting legacy to pass through generations.

One theologian said this:

> Christians ought to be celebrating constantly. We ought to be preoccupied with parties, banquets, feasts, and merriment. We ought to give ourselves over to celebrations of joy because we have been liberated from the fear of life and the fear of death. We ought to attract people to the church quite literally by the sheer pleasure there is in being a Christian.[2]

It played out just like that in the early Christian church. Remember the Festival of Weeks that you studied earlier? That feast was instructed by God to happen fifty days after Passover.

Now, you may know that Jesus was crucified around Passover time, and, of course, he was raised from the dead.

Guess how a bunch of people found out about his death and resurrection? Yep, at a party.

Fifty days after Passover, as they had done every year for a very long time, thousands of Jews gathered in Jerusalem for the Festival of Weeks—which we recognize as Pentecost in the New Testament.[*] This was a festival of thanks to God for a bountiful harvest.

While they were all gathered together, a violent wind came, flames of fire appeared over people's heads, and people began to speak in each other's languages (see Acts 2:1–13).

With a captive audience before him, Peter gave a rousing speech about the gospel—to an international audience!

A party to give thanks for the harvest of crops turned into a harvest of souls! Now, *that's* something to celebrate.

---

*It is called the day of Pentecost because it occurs fifty days after Passover.

UN-HURRY YOUR HEART

Celebrations are as old as the Bible. Feasting and dancing were a way to rehearse God's promises.

Take a moment to reflect on a favorite celebration, tradition, or holiday. How important do you think it is to set aside time to celebrate, feast, and gather with loved ones to offer gratitude?

In the previous section, I asserted that, in our modern age, we have lost the art of celebration.

If you agree with my assertion, why do you suppose that's the case?

Here's my two-part answer to that question: We think we don't have time, and we think that some things really aren't worth celebrating (such as seemingly small accomplishments or milestones reached).

As we learn to grow slow, we can recover the lost art of celebration. Let's commit to the following:

- Make intentional choices to gather, remember, and enjoy one another's company.
- Set aside time every day to catalog our thanks.
- Pause our labors to reflect on personal achievements instead of racing on to the next task.
- Stop dismissing growth as insignificant, and start seeing it as worthy of celebration.
- Create meaningful rituals in our lives to remember God's goodness.

We don't have to complicate it. Maybe we could start by lighting candles at the dinner table and slowing down enough to taste the food. Maybe we could brainstorm a way to host a Festival of Weeks party every year with friends and family. Consider reigniting a family celebration or tradition that meant something to you as a child. Start a gratitude journal. Take five minutes at the end of every day to review what you accomplished, however insignificant you think those accomplishments might be. An added benefit: Reflecting on the good stimulates the brain's reward center of your mind.

Underline at least one of the sentences in the previous paragraph as a doable way for you to incorporate more celebration in your life. Could you commit to starting one of those practices this week?

In researching celebrations of the Bible, I came across a delightful term: *love feast*. It's explicitly mentioned only one time in the New Testament, in Jude 1:12. The *Holman Illustrated Bible Dictionary* helped me understand the term more, defining it as a "fellowship meal that the Christian community celebrated with joy in conjunction with its celebration of the Lord's Supper." In the early church, it was not uncommon for small groups of friends to gather weekly for love feasts, which included hors d'oeuvres, a blessing, bread, a full meal, lively discussion, a lamplit table, a benediction, and a closing song.[3]

Could we *please* resurrect the love feast?

Have you ever experienced anything that feels a little bit like a love feast?

How could you incorporate love feasting into your life as a way to celebrate God's goodness and un-hurry your heart?

Celebrate the way that works best for you. You, my friend, are a party girl for the gospel. Of all the people on earth, we as Christians ought to be known as the ones who gather together to celebrate and live lives of joy and gratitude, because of the gift of incomparable price: the saving grace of Jesus.

PRAYER

As we close in prayer, let's remember that even when we don't see evident growth, we can celebrate the fact that God continues to grow us—even in the darkest, coldest winter seasons of our hearts. In fact, there is biblical support for celebrating and rejoicing, even in those no-growth seasons of life.

Even if the fig tree does not bloom and the vines have no grapes, even if the olive tree fails to produce and the fields yield no food, even if the sheep pen is empty and the stalls have no cattle—even then, I will be happy with the LORD. I will truly find joy in God, who saves me.

Habakkuk 3:17–18 GW

Dear Jesus,

You suffered during your time here on earth, and you also took time to celebrate. Your first miracle wasn't at a grave site; it was at a party, where you turned water to wine. You are always the life of the party, and because I belong to you, the life of the party lives in me! Help me learn to take time for celebration. Today, with a heart of celebration, I offer my gratitude for the following:

....

....

....

....

....

In your name I pray, amen.

HEAL

LEAVE NO STONE UNTURNED

But for you who revere my name, the sun of righteousness will rise with healing in its rays.

Malachi 4:2

WEEK 6 FOCUS

- to recognize the hurts that need the healing hand of God
- to lay down the burdens you've been carrying

LET'S GET STARTED

Read chapter 17 and 20 of *Growing Slow.*

Watch a free teaching video from Jennifer based on this week's session. Visit www.GrowingSlowBook.com/Resources to find the video. When prompted, enter this code for access: JDLGrowingSlow.

Last week, we were challenged to see winter as more than a dark and dreary season. Winter has gifts of its own. During winter seasons of the heart, we build strength and spiritual insights that we could not have gained any other way. Winter seasons also make space for us to recover the lost art of celebration and gratitude.

Were you able to take some time for celebration or gratitude in the past week? (See the bullet-pointed ideas in the Un-Hurry Your Heart section from the last session.) Share something about how you were intentional in this way. Remember, it could be as small as lighting candles at the dinner table.

This week we will continue to excavate the winter season for treasures to behold. I am so eager for you to dive into a final but important work on our Growing Slow journey.

My prayer is that you find both healing and rest.

MY LAND

What was your first summer job? Maybe you were a lifeguard, a waitress, or a babysitter for the young couple next door.

My first summer job: rock picker.

Every spring, local farmers would call, looking for kids to walk through their fields and "pick rock."

A bunch of us kids would sit on a flatbed trailer or hayrack while a local farmer on his tractor pulled us through his fields.

If you saw a rock, you ran after it and tossed it onto the trailer. It was an all-day job in which we covered miles of land in search of stones that, if left in the fields, would harm the field equipment during cultivating, planting, and harvest.

Looking back, the thing I find so remarkable is how the work was unending. New rocks would reappear, year after year.

How did the rocks get there? Well, there isn't some stone fairy in the sky dropping rocks on fields to annoy farmers. The rocks were there all along. You just couldn't see them. They were sitting under the surface, heaved upward in the frost/thaw cycle of the land.

My husband always tells me that winter heals the land. He says that in order for the soil to be ready for spring, it needs the cold and dark moments of winter.

It's easy to think that once everything freezes, everything is dead. That life stops. But that's not true.

There is so much happening under the soil—life and activity within microbes, hibernating animals, and worms alive and breathing beneath the surface. And then, the power of frozen ground to push a rock forth.

Winter seasons of the heart bring healing, too. Just because it's dark and dreary doesn't mean that something isn't happening inside you. Perhaps this is the time for you—like the land—to heal. For stones, long buried, to emerge.

I have long-buried stones. I talk about them on page 183 of *Growing Slow*:

> Hurtful words spoken over me when I was a child.
> Deep-seated beliefs that I'll never really be enough.
> The secret fear that I'm not lovable.
> Past sins I drag around with me because I don't fully accept
>   forgiveness or believe I'm worthy. . . .

These are my stones. They are not pretty.

My stones are heavy and jagged and ugly.

If I stay busy enough, I can keep the stones buried. But buried stones still cut the insides.

I need winter seasons of rest and quiet to bring forth the stones.

I need healing.

Maybe you do, too.

YOUR LAND

I believe that stones hide under the "soil" of each one of us. The quiet of a winter season gives us the space to allow God to do his work of pushing them forth for closer examination, in the same way stones work their way to the surface in a farmer's field.

How does that paragraph strike you? Circle the answer that most accurately describes what you're feeling.

scared, because I don't want to have to deal with stuff I've been able to hide away under the soil

weary, because I feel like my life is a constant process of dealing with some new "rock" emerging

hopeful, because maybe I can finally find freedom from unresolved burdens I've carried for too long

eager, because I regularly let winter do its work in me, and I know how much lighter I feel when stones are unearthed

_____ [Fill in the blank with a word of your choosing.]

Your stones might be tiny pebbles. Perhaps they are gigantic boulders. Some of them rose to the surface and were removed from your life long ago. But some may still be buried deep, causing lingering pain. Stones can take a lot of shapes: insecurity, loneliness, addiction, childhood trauma, sexual or domestic abuse, grief, pain, sin, unbelief, and much more. This session, we are going to unearth those stones and let Jesus do the heavy lifting.

First we will remember, and then we will retrieve.

REMEMBER

Let's take some time to remember any stones that have been unearthed in the past, resulting in true healing and freedom. No stone is too small for remembrance. This is an opportunity to call out the healing God already brought forth.

Name one or more stone in the space provided.

Remembering is an important step in spiritual growth. Remembering is a way of thanking God for how far he brought us, and how he delivered us from past hurts. We see evidence of this kind of intentional remembering in the pages of Scripture. And they did it in a most fitting way.

For example, in 1 Samuel 7, the Israelites were under attack from the Philistines, but God led them on to victory.

Read 1 Samuel 7:12 to see what Samuel did to remember God's goodness, and to remind the Israelites what the Lord had done for them. Fill in the blanks.

Then Samuel took a _____ and set it up between Mizpah and Shen. He named it _____, saying, "Thus far the Lord has _____ us."

Friend, the rocks in your fields can become your Ebenezer stones, set up as reminders that the Lord helped you. And that he won't stop helping you when new stones emerge in seasons ahead.

RETRIEVE

I believe that most—if not all—of us have other stones needing to be brought to the surface and retrieved. Most of us carry hurts that need the healing hand of God.

Where do you need to know that God will bring future healing to the field of your heart? What are the stones buried deep down, cutting and bruising and wounding your very soul? These are the stones that get in the way of your future growth. These stones keep you from healing fully and living in freedom. Do you know what these stones are?

I'm going to ask you to do a brave and beautiful thing. Take a moment and let the Holy Spirit speak to you about the stones. Maybe you need more than a moment. Maybe you need an hour or a week. Maybe you need more than this Bible study. Friend, it's more than okay if you need a mentor or a therapist to help you bring that rock to the surface so Jesus can carry it away.

No matter how big or small, would you be willing to write it here?

I hope that act brought you some measure of relief. Even in the naming, you take away some of the power that this burden has had over your life. Naming is a way of pushing the rock to the surface, in the same way that the frost/thaw cycle of winter pushes forth rocks in our fields. In the Un-Hurry Your Heart section of this session, we will gain the courage to retrieve these burdens, turning them over to God, so we can step into the freedom he offers.

HOLY LAND

Have you ever stopped to think about how much God cares about our rest and healing? He was so concerned about it that he built days of rest into the calendar as a reminder that we can take a break from our action-oriented world.

Interestingly, many of these built-in breaks happen in intervals of seven. The one that is likely most familiar to you happened at the time of creation. God was busy making the whole world and everything in it for six days, and then he rested on the seventh day. He called on his children to do the same (see Genesis 2:2–3; Exodus 23:12).

Last session, we learned about some of the festivals God ordained, and if you look back over the various festivals, you'll see that oftentimes, seven days of rest were taken.

There are more "sevens" straight ahead.

Every seventh year another kind of sabbath happens. Read Leviticus 25:4 and find out who or what this sabbath is for. Write it here.

Just like people, the land needs a break. The one-year break of the farm-land laying fallow not only was good resource management, but reminded people that God was still in charge.

Now comes a Sabbath to surpass all Sabbaths, and it has a name that makes me want to get up and dance.

Read Leviticus 25:8–13, and record the name of this year-long celebration.

You may have noticed that the festival was to take place after "seven sabbath years—seven times seven." So then, after year forty-nine, the Year of Jubilee would be celebrated every fifty years. Not only did the land rest, but the celebration was instituted to

- cancel all debts
- free all slaves
- return all land back to its original owners

Max Lucado describes the Year of Jubilee as God giving everyone a clean slate when he "shakes the social Etch A Sketch."[1]

However, "there is no indication in the Bible that the Year of Jubilee was ever carried out."[2]

Womp, womp. (Insert the sound of a sad trombone.)

But wait! As usual, Jesus brings the party back to life.

Read Luke 4:16–22 and answer the following questions:

What day did Jesus stand up and read?

What are some of the things that Jesus says he was anointed for? (See verses 18–19.)

.

After Jesus sat down, what did he tell the crowd?

Here's the kicker. When Jesus tells everybody that "this scripture is fulfilled in your hearing," he is essentially saying, "The Year of Jubilee has arrived."

Grab your air guitar and start strumming, my friend, because this is the best news—news of healing and hope that your heart might need right about now.

When Jesus spoke before that crowd, announcing the Year of Jubilee, he was telling us that he would fulfill the Year of Jubilee in the following life-altering ways:

- The Year of Jubilee was instituted to cancel financial debts. Jesus would cancel spiritual debts.
- The Year of Jubilee was instituted to free all slaves. Jesus would free us from our emotional bondage and baggage.

- The Year of Jubilee was instituted to return all land back to its original owners. Jesus will bring to us to a land beyond compare—our eternal home in heaven.

In this gigantic reset, Jesus promised full healing.

Just as the frost "heals" the land, Jesus, in his great compassion, wants to heal you and me.

> ## JUST AS THE FROST "HEALS" THE LAND, JESUS, IN HIS GREAT COMPASSION, WANTS TO HEAL YOU AND ME.

He wants to heal your brokenness, your childhood wounds, your shattered relationships. He wants to heal you from your past hurts, private addictions, and even your hurried heart.

This is our Year of Jubilee!

If Jesus were standing with you on the edge of your field today, I imagine he would leave no stone unturned.

Like we do here on the farm, he would "pick rock" until every one was carried away.

There is no rock too big, too jagged, too heavy for our Lord Jesus. How do I know?

Take note of how Jesus handled these troublesome rocks and summarize in the space provided.

John 11:38–44

John 8:3–11

John 20:1

This would be a really great spot for an "Amen" and a "Thank you, Jesus."

UN-HURRY YOUR HEART

Earlier in this session, we identified rock-like burdens that have risen up to the surface in the past. With thanksgiving, we remembered how God has healed us from past hurts, and we recounted how Samuel set up an Ebenezer stone as a reminder of God's goodness.

Then we did some soul searching to identify some of the hurts, burdens, and disappointments that are still buried deep. We named those burdens and recognized our great need for God to retrieve them.

My heart is so tender for you right now. I don't know the weight of the burdens you've been carrying, but I suspect they are heavy. I also know, from experience, that the battles you fight can exacerbate the symptoms of a hurried heart—disturbed sleep patterns, anxious thoughts, fatigue, and even physical pain. For me, the symptoms of my hurried heart are amplified when I don't want to tend to the stones in my fields, because I cope by hiding myself in productivity. Instead of letting winter do its work—slowing it all down so stones can erupt to the surface—I cram my life with busyness.

How have your burdens created a hurried heart in you? Can you name the symptoms or identify thought patterns?

Many years ago, I spoke at a Christian writers' conference in Nebraska. On a Saturday night in a little chapel, I delivered a talk that had almost nothing to do with writing or publishing. Instead, I felt led to speak about some of the burdens that get in the way of receiving God's incredible love—rejection, people pleasing, the inability to forgive, personal trauma, addiction, and much more. Yes, Christian writers struggle with all of those things.

At the end of the talk, each woman and man in the room was given a stone on which to write their burden.

As a final song played, everyone came to the front of the chapel and placed their stones in a basket. Something beautiful and holy happened. As each stone thudded upon another in the basket, people in the room began to cry and embrace one another. The simple act of naming the burden, and letting it go, set loose an emotional response that looked and sounded like freedom. I still hear from people who attended that event. They tell me that letting go of the burden was a turning point for them.

After the weekend concluded, I took all of those rocks home with me. I promised everyone that I would pray over each rock. And that's exactly what I did. I stood at the edge of a river, prayed truth and freedom over each person represented by each rock, and then I threw the rocks, one by one, into the river.

A few years later, I repeated the exercise at a retreat with Haitian women, communicating through an interpreter. Clearly, our need of rescue transcends the language barrier. Together, with tears running down our cheeks, we threw our rock burdens in the ocean.

Recently, while serving as a spiritual director at a Christian teen retreat, I repeated the exercise. At the end of the talk, teen girls and boys, in tears, dropped their burdens into a big bucket.

Here's what I have come to believe:

It doesn't matter how old you are, how young you are, how spiritual you are, how successful you are, how sinful you are, how rich you are, how poor you are, how popular you are, how put together you are, or how broken you are. Everybody is dealing with something. Everybody needs to get rid of stones in their fields.

Letting go is one of the hardest things to do. I will not minimize how difficult it is to let go of anger, sin, guilt, a relationship, trauma, regrets, hurts, and so much more.

I know that writing a burden down on a rock seems like a simple thing. I also know that some of your burdens are so heavy, so deeply ingrained, so wounding that you need something more than a pep talk from a farm girl living on the edge of a cornfield in Iowa.

But I also know that Jesus can handle any stone—no matter how deeply it's buried, no matter its size, no matter its weight.

JESUS CAN HANDLE ANY STONE—
NO MATTER HOW DEEPLY IT'S BURIED,
NO MATTER ITS SIZE,
NO MATTER ITS WEIGHT.

Read the following verses from Mark:

> And very early on the first day of the week, when the sun had risen, they
> went to the tomb. And they were saying to one another, "Who will roll away
> the stone for us from the entrance of the tomb?" And looking up, they saw
> that the stone had been rolled back—it was very large.
>
> Mark 16:2–4 ESV

How large was the stone?

Say it louder for the people in the back. *How large was that stone*?

Maybe you—like the women at the tomb—have asked yourself, *Who
will roll away this stone?* I know a guy named Jesus. He has come to retrieve your stone, and he is not intimidated by its size.

THE STONE'S THROW EXERCISE

Friend, let's lay that burden down today. I have put together this Stone's
Throw Exercise as a way for you to acknowledge and name your burden.
Then, if you're willing, I'd love for you to mail it to me so I can pray for you.

Here are some instructions for the Stone's Throw Exercise:

1. Write your burden down on the stone illustration below.

2. As you write, allow yourself to feel what you need to feel.

> Cry.
>
> Pray.
>
> Sing.
>
> Dance.
>
> Fall to your knees.
>
> Whatever you do, give yourself time and space to be present with Jesus.

3. After you write on the stone illustration provided, cut it out and mail it to me. For a printable version of the stone, visit www.Growing SlowBook.com/Resources and enter code JDLGrowingSlow. Know that I will hold your burden in my hands and will pray for you specifically. You can send your burden to me here:

> Jennifer Dukes Lee
> P.O. Box 327
> Inwood, Iowa 51240

As an alternative, ask a friend, mentor, or your Bible study leader to pray with you. There's nothing quite like an accountability partner right in your own community.

4. Ask God to roll this stone away for good and to bring freedom to your fields. Your burden may require the help of a therapist, a support group, a mentor, or a pastor. Don't hesitate to get the help your heart needs.

   (Note to Bible study leaders: You may choose to do this as a group exercise in your closing session. You can pitch actual rocks in a pond, burn the paper versions, or send them all to me! I promise to pray for every woman in your group.)

Finally, turn with me to Revelation 2:17 and read the words of Jesus. Fill in the blanks.

I will also give that person a _____ _____ with a new name written on it, known only to the one who receives it.

These mysterious verses awaken something in me. They help me to remember that Jesus knows me personally, and that when I get to heaven, every bad and ugly stone will be gone. He will hand me a white stone with a name meant just for me. I wonder if it will say *daughter* or *beloved* or *free*. Only Jesus knows the name, and because he knows the name, he knows *me*! Regular, ordinary me.

He knows you, too. Oh, friend, he knows you completely and wholly, and there's a white stone with your name on it. Someday he will hand you your stone, but until that day, write a word on this "white stone" illustration as a way to claim the freedom that is yours.

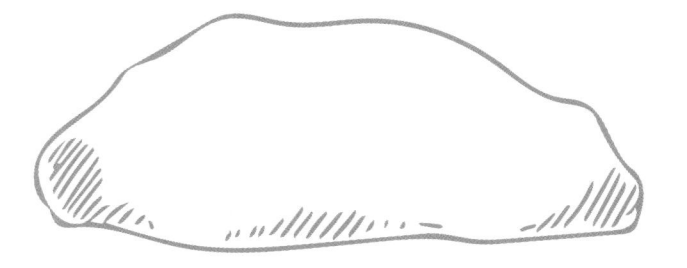

PRAYER

Throughout this study, my prayer has been that we would learn to un-hurry our hearts and fall more in love with Jesus, who was never in a hurry. May we continue to walk in the way of Growing Slow and remember that all good things—even people—take time to grow. May you "grow in the grace and knowledge of our Lord and Savior Jesus Christ. To him be glory both now and forever! Amen" (2 Peter 3:18).

In your own words, write a prayer to God, the one who loves watching you grow slow.

Epilogue

You did it! You persevered to the end. You cultivated and planted. You observed good things growing in your life, and maybe you got a foretaste of the harvest to come. You've planted so many wonderful seeds in the fields that God has given you. But make no mistake: God has planted something beautiful in you as well.

You, my friend, are a wild and glorious field, and God loves watching you grow into all that he made you to be.

Before you close this study, take a moment to reflect on how you felt at the beginning of this journey. Remember the areas of your life that had you feeling constantly rushed and in a hurry? Look how you've un-hurried your heart! Look how you've appreciated the pace and the place that God has you . . . *right now!* You are exactly where you are supposed to be.

This isn't the end of the Growing Slow journey, though. God will keep planting good seeds into you until your last breath. Keep your eyes open. Savor the beauty. Watch how beautiful growth emerges in the most unexpected fields.

I want you to know that you are worth every bit of seed planted into you.

I wish I could hug you right now. But if we don't see each other on *this* side of heaven, I'll meet you there, in the promised land.

Grow slow, my friend. Grow slow.

Leader's Guide

Thank you for stepping up to lead this *Growing Slow Bible Study*! Facilitating a group is an important commitment, but I don't want it to feel like a daunting one.

I'm guessing you said yes to this because you felt God stirring in your heart. But maybe you are wondering if you are qualified. I know how you feel! Many years ago, I began leading Bible studies in our rural Iowa community. I was so nervous and afraid I'd end up looking like a fool when I couldn't find Nehemiah or Titus in my Bible! I had so many questions about leading, and my hope is that this little guide will answer questions you may have as you lead women who desire to grow in faith alongside you.

Prayer: Starting today, commit to praying for the women who will join your study. As they begin to sign up, pray for them by name. Tape a printed list of the names inside the front of this guide. Once you begin meeting, pray for each woman every week. Consider enlisting a prayer partner to offer additional prayer support for the spoken and unspoken needs of everyone in your group. As you pray, ask the Holy Spirit to move mightily in your group, to guide you as you lead, and to reveal fresh insights to everyone.

Graphics: Several graphics are available for your use as you spread the word about your forthcoming study. We have prepared graphics for you that are perfectly sized for Instagram, Facebook cover photos, and more.

Find them all at www.GrowingSlowBook.com/Resources. The access code is JDLGrowingSlow.

Free Videos: Short teaching videos that correspond with each week's lesson are available at www.GrowingSlowBook.com/Resources. The access code is JDLGrowingSlow. You may choose to show these at the beginning of each session, or instruct the women in your group to watch them at home. This content is available to you free of charge.

First-timers: Consider inviting new people to your group, and be aware that some of them may have never attended a Bible study before. A great way to make first-timers feel welcome is to give them the workbook as a gift.

Split into groups: If more than a dozen people sign up for your study, consider dividing into smaller groups to facilitate better discussions and allow everyone to share their thoughts. The ideal size for a small group is six to ten people. Ask spiritually mature women in your group to prayerfully consider leading the groups. Ask those leaders to review this guide before the first session.

Create a comfortable environment: Plan ahead by making sure you have a distraction-free environment. Consider noise, lighting, privacy, cleanliness, and seating. Snacks and drinks are nice, but don't stress yourself out. Some fresh fruit, dark chocolate, or tortilla chips and a pitcher of ice water are adequate. If you have an especially large group, consider asking other women to take turns bringing snacks.

Let silence do its work: When facilitating sessions, be prepared for the occasional awkward silence. If you feel like the quiet in your group has gone on a bit too long, wait a few seconds longer. People often need time to formulate responses or gain the courage to speak out loud.

Affirm people: Always try to find a way to encourage those who muster up the courage to share in a group. Don't simply move on to the next question. You can affirm those who speak up by thanking them or pointing out an insightful remark they made. People are less likely to share if they feel as if you're looking only for the "right" answer.

Emphasize confidentiality: There's nothing scarier in a Bible study than sharing a deeply personal story. Remind everyone that confidentiality is expected from all.

Complete the weekly assignments: Let everyone know that they should complete the assigned week's study before you meet. Encourage them to answer all the questions in their workbooks, whether or not they choose to share them out loud with the group.

The Stone's Throw Exercise: Before you begin, study the details laid out in the Stone's Throw Exercise on pages 114–116. You may choose to do this as a group, instead of individually, to create a sense of community around the idea of giving our burdens over to Jesus.

A FRAMEWORK FOR YOUR TIME TOGETHER

You are free to lead your study at the pace you like. One possible approach: Schedule six sessions of two hours each. If you have a 7:00 p.m. start time, your evening might look like this:

7:00 p.m.	Meet, greet, and catch up with one another.
7:10 p.m.	Group prayer.
7:15 p.m.	Watch the free video available at www.GrowingSlowBook.com /Resources (access code: JDLGrowingSlow).
7:30 p.m.	Break into small groups and go through the assigned session. As a leader, you are encouraged to center your discussion on the questions in the workbook. There probably won't be time to answer all of the questions as a group, so feel free to pick the ones that might stir up the most meaningful discussion. Also, before you move on to the next section or page, consider asking the group, "Was there anything else on this page that you would like to discuss?"
8:30 p.m.	Take prayer requests from members of your small group. Pray specifically for individual requests.

8:50 p.m. Remind participants to
- complete the next assignment
- complete the assigned readings from *Growing Slow*
- continue to hold one another up in prayer through the week

8:55 p.m. Dismiss your group.

God has equipped you for this!

Notes

Week One: Notes

1. Paul H. Wright, *Understanding the Ecology of the Bible: An Introductory Atlas* (Jerusalem: Carta, 2018), 6.

Week Two: Notes

1. Living life "as if you are afraid of being late to your own funeral" is a quote from Geir Berthelsen, "Ten-Point Guide to Going Slow," World Institute of Slowness, accessed November 19, 2020, https://www.theworldinstituteofslowness.com/geir-berthelsens-ten -point-guide-to-going-slow/.
2. Online Etymology Dictionary, s.v. "slow," accessed November 19, 2020, https:// www.etymonline.com/word/slow.
3. Faisal Hoque, "Five Ways Working More Slowly Can Boost Your Productivity," *Fast Company*, March 18, 2016, https://www.fastcompany.com/3057853/five-ways-working -more-slowly-can-boost-your-productivity.
4. Sandi Mann, Rebekah Cadman, "Does Being Bored Make Us More Creative?," *Creativity Research Journal* 26, no. 2 (May 18, 2014): 165–173, https://doi.org/10.1080 /10400419.2014.901073.

Week Three: Notes

1. Frederick Buechner, "The Stewardship of Pain," sermon on *Chicago Sunday Evening Club TV Program*, January 27, 1991, https://www.youtube.com/watch?v=73hdH1_z2ps.
2. Study notes on Genesis 39:20, *NIV Life Application Study Bible*, 3rd. ed. (Carol Stream, IL: Tyndale; Grand Rapids, MI: Zondervan, 2019), 74.
3. The prayer is most often attributed to the writer Robin Fogle.

Week Four: Notes

1. This quote is often attributed to William J. Toms.

2. Jerry Root, "How Can We Overcome Our Fear of Evangelism?," The Exchange with Ed Stetzer, *Christianity Today*, August 7, 2018, https://www.christianitytoday.com /edstetzer/2018/august/how-can-we-overcome-our-fear-of-evangelism.html.

Week Five: Notes

1. Charles H. Spurgeon, "To Those Who Feel Unfit for Communion," *The Metropolitan Tabernacle Pulpit Sermons*, vol. 36 (London: Passmore & Alabaster, 1823), 490.

2. Robert Hotchkins, quoted in Randy Alcorn, "Christianity Is Not a Frowning Contest," The Gospel Coalition, October 16, 2019, https://www.thegospelcoalition.org/article /win-them-frowns/.

3. *Holman Illustrated Bible Dictionary* (Nashville: Holman Bible Publishers, 2003), 1055–1056.

Week Six: Heal: Leave No Stone Unturned

1. Max Lucado, *Outlive Your Life: You Were Made to Make a Difference* (Nashville: Thomas Nelson, 2010), 103.

2. Study notes from *Life Application Study Bible* on Leviticus 25:8–17, *NLT Parallel Study Bible* (Carol Stream, IL: Tyndale, 2011), 221.

Jennifer Dukes Lee is the author of *Growing Slow*, *It's All Under Control*, *The Happiness Dare*, and *Love Idol*. She is also a writer for Dayspring's (in)courage, and a speaker at women's events across the United States. Her words have been featured on numerous podcasts, radio programs, and other outlets, including Proverbs 31 Ministries, Fox News's *Opinion*, the *Des Moines Register*, and *Today's Christian Woman*.

Jennifer is known for her authentic voice as she encourages women to walk in freedom. She clings to the hope of the cross and is passionate about sharing the gospel through story. She believes in miracles; she is one. She marvels at God's unrelenting grace for people who mess up—stumbling sinners like her, who have been made whole through Christ.

Jennifer and her husband live on the Lee family farm in Iowa, where they raise crops, pigs, and two beautiful humans. She attends a small country church, where some Sundays you'll find her spinning tunes as the church DJ. She's a big fan of dark chocolate, emojis, eighties music, bright lipstick, and Netflix binges. She wants to live her life in such a way that you can't help but want more of Jesus.

Connect with Jennifer

jenniferdukeslee.com

@JenniferDukesLee

@jenniferdukeslee

More from Jennifer Dukes Lee

We long to take a break from the fast pace of life, but we're afraid of what we'll miss if we do. Yet when hustling hard leaves us stressed, perhaps this is our cue to step into a more sustainable pace. In this inspiring read, Jennifer Dukes Lee offers a path to unhurried living by returning to the rhythm of the land and learning the ancient art of *Growing Slow*.

Growing Slow

BETHANY HOUSE

Stay up to date on your favorite books and authors with our free e-newsletters. Sign up today at bethanyhouse.com.

 facebook.com/BHPnonfiction

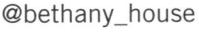 @bethany_house

 @bethany_house_nonfiction